MYRNA OAKLEY

A Voyager Book

Old Saybrook, Connecticut

Library of Congress Cataloging-in-Publication Data
Oakley, Myrna.
Oregon : off the beaten path / by Myrna Oakley. — 2nd ed.
p. cm.
"A Voyager book."
Includes index.
ISBN 1-56440-495-1
1. Oregon—Guidebooks. I. Title.
F874.3.024 1994
917.9504'43—dc20
94-27159
CIP

Manufactured in the United States of America
Second Edition/First Printing

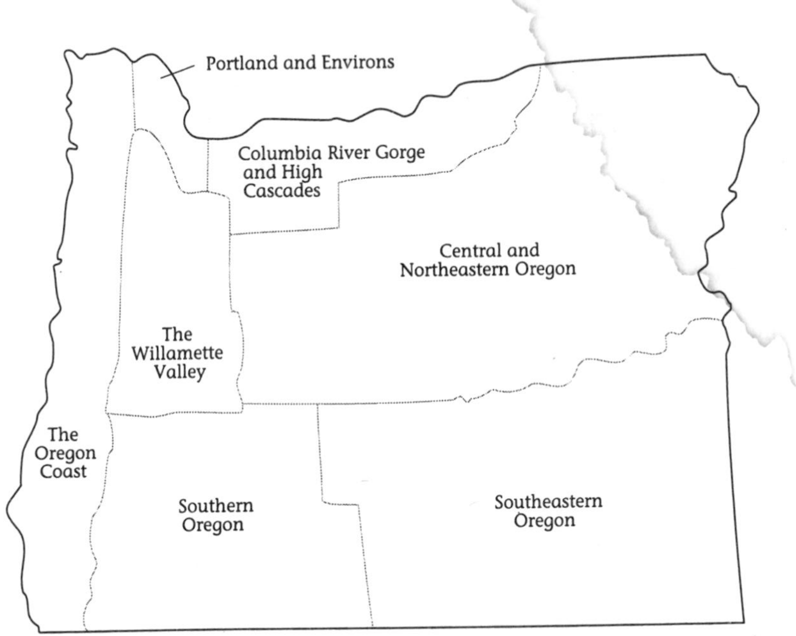
OREGON
Portland and Environs
Columbia River Gorge and High Cascades
Central and Northeastern Oregon
The Willamette Valley
The Oregon Coast
Southern Oregon
Southeastern Oregon

CONTENTS

To Bradford, P.J., and Marisa, who have yet to discover the joys of traveling off the beaten path

Introduction

Looking back a few years ago, I remember fully discovering—and truly appreciating—the vast, diverse character of my native Oregon in the late 1960s and early 1970s, when I traveled with some forty-seven seventh-graders, several fellow teachers, and helpful parents on working field trips throughout the Beaver State.

On the Oregon coast we found eons-old seashell fossils and explored driftwood-strewn beaches and brimming tide pools; on the high desert east of the rugged Cascade Mountains we visited ancient volcano remnants, lava caves, and lava-cast forests; and we identified all the life zones, trees, vegetation, and wildflowers in between.

We trekked into the Columbia River Gorge and hiked past waterfalls and into narrow chasms, peering at thick layers of volcanic basalt supporting colonies of licorice fern, colorful lichens and mosses, and dozens of native wildflowers.

We marveled at the wide Columbia River, along whose banks Native American families fished and traded for thousands of years, the place where the first Oregon Trail pioneers, in 1843, floated belongings down the rampaging river to sites near Fort Vancouver, Oregon City, and, later, Portland.

On the high desert near Bend we camped for four days and held school under the wide blue sky beneath pungent junipers on one day, then under tall, cinnamon-barked ponderosa pine on another. Surrounded by yellow blooming sagebrush, low-growing manzanita, bitterbrush, and wide-open vistas in every direction, we absorbed a new awareness of the outdoors, a new appreciation of nature's life cycles.

Some seven or eight students, arms outstretched and hands clasped, encircled an enormous ponderosa pine tree near LaPine and the Little Deschutes River. From atop Lava Butte we viewed the Cascade's highest snowcapped volcanic peaks—Mt. Washington, Mt. Jefferson, Three-Fingered Jack, Mt. Bachelor, the Three Sisters, and Mt. Hood.

With flashlights and lanterns we explored cavernous lava tubes—Skeleton Cave and Lava River Cave. We peered down into Arnold Ice Cave and learned that early Oregon pioneers chopped huge blocks of ice there and hauled them by horse-and-buggy to Bend for refrigeration.

At Fort Rock, an enormous volcanic remnant, we found nesting baby eagles and marveled at towering, wave-cut ledges created by ancient seas. At night, under a canopy of glittering stars, we sat around the campfire and listened to the spine-tingling poetic tales of Robert Service.

By now, traveling off the beaten path has become a well-worn habit, one shared by many fellow Oregonians as well as visitors. Our wide ocean beaches and spectacular coastline remain a favorite destination—fully preserved for everyone to enjoy. A sense of the mid-1840s pioneer past still permeates much of the state, and sections of the Oregon Trail, including the actual wagon ruts, have been identified and preserved in eastern and central Oregon.

Communities throughout the state welcome visitors to local history society museums, living history programs, and vintage homes and gardens where glimpses of Oregon's pioneer past can be seen and appreciated. Many covered bridges—and lighthouses, along the entire Oregon coast—have been preserved and can be easily located.

The safekeeping of early Oregon farms and homesteads is a continuing priority, and the battles over the protection of old-growth Douglas fir forests, as well as setting aside natural wildlife and bird-life areas to conserve them from overdevelopment, takes on that independent pioneer spirit so deeply ingrained here.

Regardless of how far off the beaten path you travel in Oregon, you'll also discover coastal and mountain lodges, inviting bed-and-breakfast inns, elegant destination resorts, quaint shops, regional vineyards and wineries, and unique eateries. I hope you enjoy this personal field trip through the Beaver State—walking in the footsteps of yesterday as well as today.

To aid you in planning your travels, a list of resources is included following the last chapter. As this book goes to press, all information is current. Should you discover other uncommon places in Oregon to recommend for future editions, please drop me a line in care of The Globe Pequot Press, P.O. Box 833, Old Saybrook, Connecticut 06475. Happy travels!

The prices and rates listed in this guidebook were confirmed at press time. We recommend, however, that you call establishments before traveling to obtain current information.

The Oregon Coast

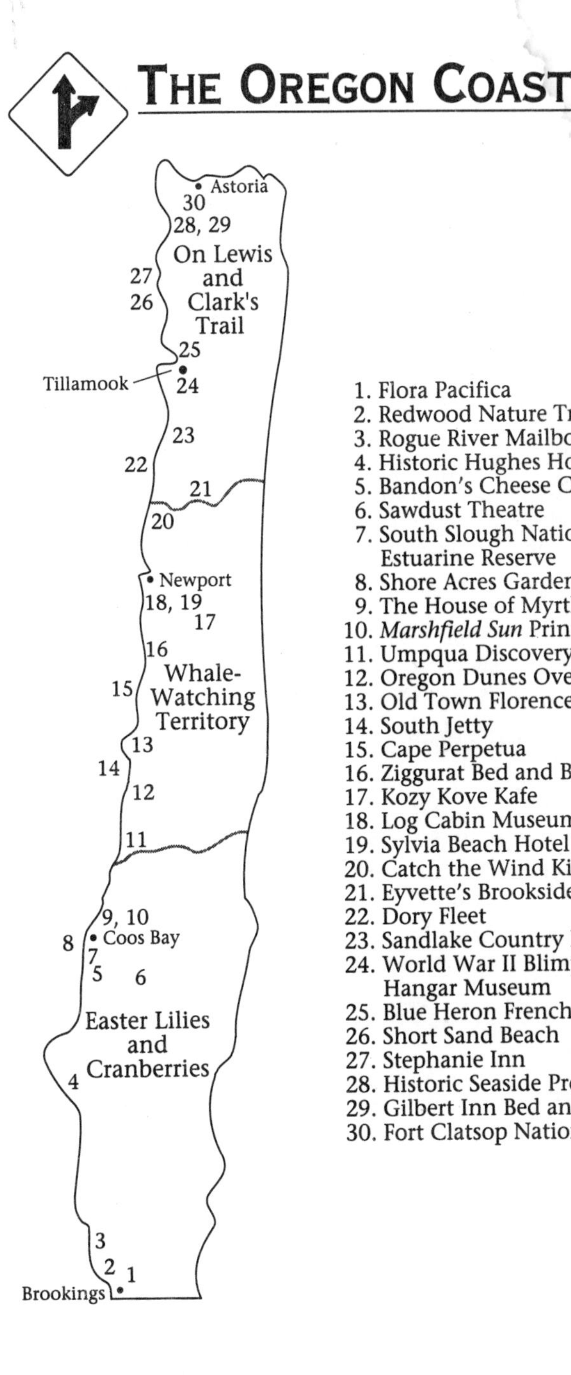

1. Flora Pacifica
2. Redwood Nature Trail
3. Rogue River Mailboat Trips
4. Historic Hughes House
5. Bandon's Cheese Company
6. Sawdust Theatre
7. South Slough National Estuarine Reserve
8. Shore Acres Gardens
9. The House of Myrtlewood
10. *Marshfield Sun* Printing Museum
11. Umpqua Discovery Center
12. Oregon Dunes Overlook
13. Old Town Florence
14. South Jetty
15. Cape Perpetua
16. Ziggurat Bed and Breakfast
17. Kozy Kove Kafe
18. Log Cabin Museum
19. Sylvia Beach Hotel
20. Catch the Wind Kite Shop
21. Eyvette's Brookside Cafe
22. Dory Fleet
23. Sandlake Country Inn
24. World War II Blimp Hangar Museum
25. Blue Heron French Cheese Factory
26. Short Sand Beach
27. Stephanie Inn
28. Historic Seaside Promenade
29. Gilbert Inn Bed and Breakfast
30. Fort Clatsop National Monument

The Oregon Coast

Easter Lilies and Cranberries

With its mild, relatively dry winters, the southern Oregon coast offers many appealing options—clamming, crabbing, hiking, fishing, beachcombing, museum hopping, and just plain solitude beckon visitors to linger awhile.

From late June to early September, fields of lilies, both Easter lilies and Oriental hybrids, nod in colorful profusion, and travelers can detour from coastal Highway 101 just south of Brookings to see them, at **Strahm's Lilies** and at **Flora Pacifica,** 15447 Ocean View Drive, Harbor 97415 (503–469–9741). Enjoy the viewing garden and several acres of flowers for cutting, such as calla lilies, astilbe, delphinium, and larkspur. You can see where the flowers are dried and made into natural swags and wreaths as well as browse the gift shop Wednesday through Saturday from 11:00 A.M. to 5:00 P.M.

You can then head out the Chetco River Road and spend an hour or so hiking the 1-mile **Redwood Nature Trail,** located a half-mile north of Alfred A. Loeb State Park, on the north bank of the Chetco River. Aided by the helpful interpretive brochure, you'll pass some fourteen numbered stations and identify trees, shrubs, ferns, and flowers that are characteristic of this coastal region. The large redwoods range between 300 and 800 years in age and may reach heights of 350 feet and girths of 25 feet.

Notice also the tanoak, a broadleaf tree that often grows with redwood. At one time tannin from the peeled bark of the tanoak was used by the Pacific Coast leather industry. You'll also identify the black huckleberry, which has bluish black fruit, and the red huckleberry, which has bright red, tart berries. Both make delicious jelly.

Note: This nature trail is moderately difficult, as some sections are steep, but there are benches along the way. Be sure to wear sturdy shoes.

For other wilderness hiking information, stop by the Chetco Ranger Station in Brookings, at 555 Fifth Street (503–469–2196). Ask about the several recreational rentals, including the **Packer's Cabin,** for primitive overnight adventures in the heart of the Chetco River forest area. This cozy cabin, located 20 miles east of town, has a wood stove, but you bring in your own water, food, and bedding.

Guided rafting and drift-boat fishing trips are also available on the Chetco River; information about local guides can be obtained from the ranger station or from the Brookings-Harbor Visitors' Information Center, P.O. Box 940, Brookings 97415 (503–469–3181).

Because this sort of invigorating outdoor activity often develops ravenous appetites, you might want to stop at **Plum Pudding Restaurant** for breakfast or lunch before heading into the coastal wilderness areas. From enormous omelets—served with sour cream and cheese potatoes and grainy nut bread—to grilled roast beef sandwiches, seafoods, and triple chocolate tortes, travelers are welcomed at this well-known eatery at 1011 Chetco Avenue in Brookings. The establishment is open for breakfast and lunch Monday through Saturday (503–469–6961).

History buffs may want to plan a visit to the **Chetco Valley Historical Society Museum,** located in the oldest standing house in the Brookings-Harbor area. The vintage red-and-white structure served as a stagecoach station on the south coast during the early 1800s. On display are World War II artifacts, old photographs, and a quilt collection that includes a pioneer quilt made in 1844. The museum is located at 15461 Museum Road, 2 miles south of Brookings; its telephone number is (503) 469–6651. Notice the enormous Monterey cypress in front of the museum; one of the largest in the United States, it's 99 feet tall and measures more than 30 feet around the massive trunk. The museum is open May through October on Tuesday through Saturday from 2:00 to 6:00 P.M. and November through April on Sunday from noon to 5:00 P.M.

If time permits, detour at **Cape Sebastion,** located just north of Brookings and Pistol River, some 5 miles south of Gold Beach. Rising 500 feet from the salty Pacific Ocean, the cape offers spectacular wide-angle views of the coastline north and south, as well as hiking trails and picnic areas. Don't be deterred by the weather; this sight is not to be missed, even on a blustery day.

For one of the best side trips on the south Curry coast, take one of the ◆**Rogue River Mailboat Trips** up the lower Rogue River. Here, passengers and mail are transported in open and safe hydrojet-powered launches across ripples and easy rapids about

32 miles upriver, to Agness. Good-natured pilots point out wildlife and geological features along the way, often recounting lively tales of early river life.

Some call it Zane Grey country, for the fabled writer of westerns had a cabin in the area, where he came to fish and write in the solitude of the rushing river and forests of giant Douglas fir. A hearty lunch at rustic **Singing Springs Lodge** and the 32-mile return trip to Gold Beach complete this memorable trip into the Rogue River's pioneer past. Information about the mailboat trips can be obtained from the Gold Beach–Wedderburn Visitors' Information Center, 1225 South Ellensburg, Gold Beach 97444 (503–247–7526). A longer, 102-mile, round-trip excursion up into the federally designated Wild and Scenic section of the Rogue River is also available.

As you head north on Highway 101, the coastal headlands press close to the ocean, and the highway, once a narrow Indian trail, curves along a shelf high above the waves and around Humbug Mountain to Port Orford. In 1828 mountain man Jedediah Smith trekked through the area with a dozen men and 150 horses loaded with furs obtained by trapping and trading in California. Crossing the mouth of the Rogue River, Jedediah reported in his journal that twelve horses drowned but the furs, ferried across in canoes, were saved.

At Port Orford visit the local harbor, a natural deep-water area where fishing boats are hoisted in and out of the churning waters each day with an enormous converted log boom. You'll often see the boats resting high and dry on long trailers atop the pier.

For hearty family fare stop at **Whale Cove Restaurant,** just off Highway 101 in Port Orford. The new owners serve breakfast, lunch, and dinner daily (503–332–7575), offering vegetarian items as well as enormous hamburgers and fresh-cooked hash browns.

If time allows, drive about 5 miles west of Highway 101—just north of Port Orford—to **Cape Blanco State Park** to see the **Cape Blanco Lighthouse.** Constructed in the 1870s, the lighthouse is one of the best-known landmarks to ships that ply the ocean both north and south of Port Orford. It is now closed to the public. Nearby, the restored ◆ **Historic Hughes House,** circa 1898, sits on a bank above the winding Sixes River. It was built by pioneers Patrick and Jane Hughes thirty years after they'd bought the land and started a dairy ranch. Now part of the Cape

Blanco State Park complex, the house is open from May to September on Wednesday through Saturday from 10:00 A.M. to 5:00 P.M. and on Sunday from noon to 5:00 P.M. The turnoff to the house is about 4 miles out Cape Blanco Road.

Of the nine original lighthouses on the Oregon coast, light beams from six of them continue to guide mariners, fishing parties, sailors, and pleasure boaters along coastal waters. Although newer technology in marine navigation—radiobeacons and such—has retired the other three lighthouses from active service, there is growing interest in preserving these vintage maritime structures as historic sites, interpretive centers, and museums.

The nearby **Sixes River** offers fishing for fall chinook, spring and fall sea-run cutthroat, and winter steelhead. **Cape Blanco State Park** is open from April to November and has complete facilities for day and overnight use, in addition to a primitive hiker-biker camp. A helpful booklet on Oregon's state parks and campgrounds can be obtained from the State Parks and Recreation Division, 525 Trade Street South East, Salem 97310 (503–379–6305). *Note:* There are large state campgrounds in each section of the coast that remain open all year.

In tiny Sixes, 5 miles north of Port Orford, the historic **Sixes River Hotel,** recently renovated, has developed a following for both its small restaurant and its cozy guest rooms. Owner and chef Marilyn Dewitt serves such tasty entrées as pork tenderloin with orange sauce and wasabi butter, ling cod with baby shrimp sauce, and tortellini with prawns. Everything served is fresh, including the meats, seafood, and vegetables. The dining room is open Wednesday through Saturday, 6:00–9:00 P.M., and on Sunday for brunch, 10:00 A.M.–2:00 P.M. Call (503) 332–3900 for information and reservations.

Located at the mouth of the Coquille River, where the river surges into the Pacific Ocean, the community of Bandon is known for its cheese and its cranberries. Milk for the original Bandon Cheese and Produce Company, founded in 1927, was hauled from nearby Coquille Valley dairies by stern-wheel riverboats, and both cheddar cheese and butter were shipped to San Francisco by steamboat.

Stop at ◆ **Bandon's Cheese Company** (503–347–2456), located on Highway 101, where you can see the "cheddaring" process take place in long stainless-steel vats. Large bricks of curd are carefully flipped over and over, then stacked to allow the whey to drain so that the curd can reach its optimum cheddar texture. In the gourmet gift shop, you can sample an assortment of mouth-watering varieties—from Medium and aged Sharp Cheddar to a zingy Jalapeño Jack.

Then, too, some 900 acres of cranberry bogs are under cultivation near Bandon. The original vines were brought from Cape Cod, Massachusetts, in 1879 by pioneer grower Charles McFarlin. In those days the Coos Indians helped pick the bright red berries with wooden-toothed scoops each autumn. The Bandon community celebrates a cranberry festival each September.

Displays of Indian artifacts and old photos of the cranberry harvest, as well as exhibits of local history—the town burned to the ground twice, in 1914 and 1936—can be seen at the **Bandon Historical Museum,** near the harbor and **Old Town.** Located in a large old U.S. Coast Guard building, the museum is open Tuesday through Sunday from 10:00 A.M. to 4:00 P.M. and is well worth a stop. Call (503) 687–4239 for additional information.

Within walking distance of the museum, you can enjoy a stroll through Old Town shops and galleries. On Baltimore Street the bulletin board outside **Andrea's Restaurant**—a favorite with the locals—usually lists the current schedule for the **Bandon Storm Watchers.** Beginning in January, this group of storm lovers hosts a series of a dozen or more enrichment programs on Saturdays at 3:00 P.M. at the Bandon Community Center in City Park. From "Watching Sea Birds" to "Whales and Their Eating Habits" to "Tide Pools at Low Tide," the programs feature slide shows and lectures by local experts and provide an opportunity for you to mingle with friendly Bandon folks. For your own copy of the current schedule, write the Bandon Storm Watchers at P.O. Box 1515, Bandon 97411 (503–347–9616).

For a pleasant side trip from Bandon, head east on Highway 42 for about 15 miles to Coquille, where you can take in an old-fashioned melodrama, such as *Sweet, Sweet Revenge* or *Live Women in the Mines,* at the ◆ **Sawdust Theatre** on Saturday evenings at 8:00 P.M. during June and on Fridays and Saturdays from July through Labor Day. The community's annual Gay 90's Celebration on the first Saturday of June launches the summer season. For information call the Coquille Visitor's Center, (503) 396–3414. Tickets to the vintage melodrama go on sale starting March 15 (503–396–4563).

From Highway 101 again, detour about 10 miles north of Bandon onto Seven Devils Road toward Charleston to find the **South Slough National Estuarine Reserve,** a 4,400-acre natural preserve. You can walk the nature trail near the Interpretive Center or try one of the longer trails that loop through upland forest, salt marshes, tide flats, and open-water zones. During summer months you can take informative workshops on wildflowers, edible plants, and local birds.

The Interpretive Center (503–888–5558) features colorful displays and a good selection of nature books about the estuary. It is open weekdays September through May and open every day June through August, 8:30 A.M.–4:30 P.M. If you have your own canoe and gear and want to paddle through the slough's quiet waters, ask about nearby canoe launch areas. Ask, too, about guided canoe tours and guided nature walks.

To experience some magnificent but often overlooked coastal scenery, detour from Highway 101 about 10 miles north of Bandon to Charleston and then double back to Sunset Bay, Shore Acres, and Cape Arago. This area can also be accessed from Coos Bay–North Bend, farther north.

Sandstone cliffs curve around picturesque, half-moon **Sunset Bay,** atop which are easy hiking trails. At low tide walk out along the rocks on the south side to explore tide pools filled with sea anemones, tiny crab, oblong chiton, and purple sea urchins. Wear sturdy shoes for this trek so as not to take a spill on wet rocks and slippery seaweed.

There are a shady picnic area, a large overnight campground, and a safe, sandy beach at Sunset Bay. Plan to spend an hour or so visiting nearby **Shore Acres Gardens,** once the grand estate of a wealthy south coast lumberman, Louis J. Simpson, whose prospering business had been built by his father, Asa Meade Simpson, in the late 1800s. The garden is just a mile beyond Sunset Bay.

A wooded walkway invites visitors past a display illustrating the history of Shore Acres and the Simpson family, researched by Oregon historian Stephen Dow Beckham. The garden features enormous beds of elegant roses, lush plantings of dahlias, exotic tree species, and a lovely sunken Japanese Garden. Along the nearby sea cliff is an enclosed gazebo where the mansion once perched—an excellent place to watch for whales and to safely view the crashing waves of winter storms. Notice, too, the uptilted ledges and massive outcroppings—ancient geology at its best on the south coast!

Easy hiking trails and picnic areas are also available on the grounds. The park is open year-round from dawn to dusk and is decorated with thousands of lights from the second week in December through New Year's Eve.

Drive on to **Cape Arago,** at the end of the road, for another panorama of wave-sculpted bluffs, for ocean breezes, and, often, for the cacophony of barking Steller sea lions, harbor seals, and elephant seals, on Simpson's Reef. You'll find secluded picnic tables and hiking trails here as well. Year-round camping is also available at nearby **Bastendorff Beach County Park,** along with a wide sandy beach and good views of the ocean.

Heading past the county park back toward Coos Bay–North Bend, notice the colorful boat harbor at **Charleston;** here visitors can go crabbing from the dock area. A small visitors' center near the bridge is open during summer and can provide information about crab nets and bait; call (503) 888–2311. Charter fishing excursions are also available at the Charleston Marina.

If you're hungry for seafood and haven't the time to catch your own, stop at **Mo's Restaurant,** located at 700 South Broadway in Coos Bay, for delicious clam chowder, slumgullion, or tasty fish-and-chips. If your taste buds cater to more natural foods, try the **Blue Heron Bistro,** which is well-known for home-baked breads, tasty soups, delicious entrées, freshly made desserts, and gourmet coffee. The cafe, located at the corner of Commercial and Highway 101, is open daily from 9:00 A.M. to 9:00 P.M. (except major holidays).

For a tour through one of the south coast's myrtlewood factories, stop at ◆**The House of Myrtlewood,** at the south edge of Coos Bay. You can tour the factory, watch the production process, and see local artisans create polished bowls, trays, cups, and other handcrafted gift items from the rough myrtlewood logs.

As an added treat, the House of Myrtlewood folks make more than twelve varieties of cream and butter fudge—be sure to ask for a taste of your favorite. The gift shop also stocks many Northwest wines and an assortment of local and regional gourmet foods. Ask about the selection of Cozette's gourmet goodies, including cranberry marmalade, brandied cranberries, and cranberry hazelnut compote with rum. The factory and gift shop are open every day (except Christmas, New Year's, and Thanksgiving) from 8:00 A.M. to 5:00 P.M.; call (503) 267–7804 for more information. And to obtain a catalog, write to the factory at P.O. Box 457, Coos Bay 97420.

For a visit to a historic newspaper and job-printing shop on the National Register of Historic Places, plan a summertime stop at the ◆***Marshfield Sun* Printing Museum,** located at the corner of Front Street and Bayshore Drive (Highway 101) in Coos Bay. The *Marshfield Sun* newspaper was edited and published by Jesse Allen Luse from 1891 until 1944. You'll see a Washington handpress, a Chandler and Price platen press, and nearly 200 type cases and fonts of type on the main floor of the museum. On the upper level are exhibits on the history of printing and on early Marshfield, which was Coos Bay's former name, as well as a collection of old U.S. newspapers. The museum is open during the summer on Tuesday through Saturday from 1:00 to 4:00 P.M. Special open-house tours are also scheduled during the year, and a guided tour can be arranged by calling the Bay Area Visitors' Information Center at (503) 269–0215 or at the toll-free number, (800) 824–8486.

On the outskirts of North Bend, history buffs can stop at the **Coos-Curry Pioneer and Historical Association Museum** at Simpson Park for a look at south coast Indian and pioneer displays, exhibits, and vintage books and scrapbooks. On the grounds you'll see an old-time railroad steam engine and antique logging equipment. Just next door is the well-stocked North Bend Visitors' Information Center, along with a shady picnic area and public rest rooms. The museum is open May through September on Tuesday through Saturday from 10:00 A.M. to 4:00 P.M. and on Sunday from 1:00 to 4:00 P.M.; call the museum at (503) 756–6320 to make arrangements to visit during winter months.

Heading north from Coos Bay–North Bend, you'll drive high above the bay via **McCullough Bridge,** one of the longest bridges constructed by the Works Progress Administration along the Oregon coast. Signed into law by President Franklin D. Roosevelt, the Works Progress Administration projects provided much-needed work for thousands of Americans during the Great Depression. McCullough Bridge is nearly a mile in length and was dedicated on June 5, 1936. The channel spans rise 150 feet to accommodate ships entering and leaving Coos Bay's large protected harbor.

Motoring with ease, one forgets that scenic Highway 101, with its many bridges spanning numerous rivers, was once a windswept wilderness laced with deer and Indian trails. In the 1800s both Indians and explorers traveled on foot, on horseback, by canoe, and, later, by ferry.

Actually, the journals of early mountain man Jedediah Smith and explorer Alexander McLeod often reported progress of less than 5 miles a day through thick coastal forests, over rugged ravines and valleys, and across rushing streams, rivers, and bays. Later, a stage-line route along the beach was established and remained in use until 1916. The stage operated on a "flexible" schedule—determined by the incoming or outgoing tide!

Just off Highway 101, heading north toward Winchester Bay and Reedsport, detour to Lakeside and the **Tenmile Lakes** area. A small community often overlooked, Lakeside traces its settlement to the 1850s, when "Ten Mile Tom," a Native American, is said to have built the first permanent cabin along the lakeshore. In the early 1900s the Southern Pacific railway ran a "fisherman's special" train on weekends with a stop at Lakeside.

Much of North as well as South Tenmile Lake is still accessible only by boat, its many arms reaching into Coastal Range forests. Anglers return year after year to stalk the black bass, bluegill, trout, and catfish in the lake's waters. Good boat ramps, a marina, art boutiques, motels, and campgrounds are found here; ask, too, about floating houseboat rentals and the annual bass-fishing contest held each spring. Further information can be obtained from the Lakeside Visitors' Information Center, P.O. Box 333, Lakeside 97449 (503–759–3011).

WHALE-WATCHING TERRITORY

Travel north again on Highway 101 to **Winchester Bay,** the largest salmon-fishing harbor on the Oregon coast, and discover bustling **Salmon Harbor**—where the Umpqua River meets the Pacific Ocean—by turning west toward **Windy Cove Campground.** You'll find facilities here for launching seaworthy boats and for renting crabbing and fishing equipment; you'll also find

Salmon Harbor

custom canning, bait, fuel, and ice, as well as information about appropriate fishing licenses.

Charter deep-sea fishing trips are available throughout most of the year at Salmon Harbor; call the harbor office (503–271–3407) or the Lower Umpqua Visitors' Center (800–247–2155) for information and current schedules.

At Reedsport you can walk along reconstructed boardwalks that are reminiscent of the industrial area that housed canneries and sawmill sheds in earlier days, and learn about the small coastal town's history at the new **Umpqua Discovery Center.** The kids will enjoy peeking through the center's periscope for a 360-degree view of the Umpqua River, nearby railroad swing bridge, and jet-boat dock. You can also tour the 125-foot polar research sailing vessel, *Hero,* permanently moored here as part of an Antarctic exhibit. The center is open 10:00 A.M.–6:00 P.M. from May 15 to September 30; winter hours are 10:00 A.M.–4:00 P.M. except Mondays and Tuesdays. Snacks are available at the Schooner Cafe on the boardwalk. You can also explore the scenic Umpqua River, home to bald eagles, many gamefish species, and protected Roosevelt elk, on the 680-horsepower jet boat, *Miss Umpqua,* during summer months. For further information call the Lower Umpqua Visitors' Center in Reedsport at (800) 247–2155.

For a look into the archaeological past, about 8,000 years ago, plan another side trip from Highway 101 to visit the **Tahkenitch Landing Archaeological Site** located next to Tahkenitch Campground. Interpretive signs at the site help you imagine the area where Native American families hunted and fished in eons past. Find the all-weather road just north of Reedsport and Gardiner and enjoy a 6½-mile drive into the cool, green Siuslaw National Forest to the campground. Tahkenitch Lake encompasses about 115 miles of shoreline.

Just south of Florence, detour at the **Oregon Dunes Overlook,** a scenic pullout area whose handicap-accessible observation decks offer good views of the ocean and dunes. In the Oregon Dunes are twelve developed trails, ranging from a ¾-mile stroll along a small lagoon to a 6-mile hike through Douglas fir forests and rugged dunes. Maps and information can be obtained from the well-stocked Oregon Dunes National Recreation Area Headquarters, 855 Highway 101, Reedsport 97467 (503–271–3611).

At the junction of Highway 101 and Highway 126, near the mouth of the Siuslaw River, stop and explore Florence, a thriving community of some 5,000 coast dwellers. **Old Town Florence,** along the river near Bay Street, is a pleasant place to stroll and poke into charming shops, galleries, and eateries housed in some of the town's most historic buildings.

For a look at the oldest structure, walk a block or so to the corner of First and Maple streets to see the **Johnson House,** a large, two-story, white saltbox-style house that is nearly a hundred years old. Now completely renovated, it's open to travelers as a bed-and-breakfast inn, Florence's first. Along Bay Street, in Old Town, shop and eat at **Traveler's Cove Cafe & Gift Shop;** enjoy great sundaes and cones at **BJ's Ice Cream;** have tea and scones at **Old English Tea Company;** or stop in for a steaming cup of espresso or cappuccino at **Old Town Coffee Company.** It's just across the street from the Kite Shop and an old-fashioned gazebo in tiny **Old Town Park,** where you can sit with a view of the Siuslaw River and its vintage bridge, circa 1936, constructed by the Works Progress Administration.

If you haven't time to try catching your own crab but would like to see how it's done, drive to the **South Jetty,** walk out on the large wooden pier, and watch folks lower bait-filled crab rings into the churning waters. Here you're on the Siuslaw River estuary, where the river meets the Pacific Ocean—surging mightily against the oncoming tides. *Siuslaw* is an Indian word meaning "far away waters." Most of the lakes in the area have special Indian names: *Cleawox,* meaning "paddle wood"; *Siltcoos,* meaning "plenty elk"; and *Tahkenitch,* meaning "many arms."

On the way out to the jetty, just south of Florence and off highway 101, you'll pass large sand dunes and several parking areas for beach access. The flat access road, away from busy Highway 101, is also good for bicycling. To see more than 200 snowy-white tundra swans that winter here November through February, walk from the third beach parking area onto a dirt road that leads to the wildlife-viewing levee. The swans, with 6-foot wingspans, long necks, and black beaks, nibble on aquatic leaves and tubers in the river's marshes. *Note:* It's a good idea to bring rain gear, waterproof boots, and binoculars.

If you'd just as soon ride a horse as a bicycle, check with the friendly folks at **C and M Stables,** located 8 miles north of Florence at 90241 Highway 101 North, to reserve a gentle steed for beach and sunset rides, dune trail rides, or winter rides. On a trusty mount follow the trail through a lush alder forest down to the dunes and beach, perhaps spying deer, ducks, swans, and geese in the dune marsh areas along the way. You might even see a stately Roosevelt elk or an elusive coyote. For reservations call

(503) 997–7540. The stables are open daily from June through October but closed on Mondays and Tuesdays during winter months. Call ahead from Florence for reservations.

Before continuing on, stop and say hello to owners Elise and Dale Center at **Woodsman Native Nursery,** just 2 miles north of Florence, to refill your picnic basket with their wide selection of wild jams and jellies: native raspberry, blueberry, wild huckleberry, and elderberry, as well as native blackberry, cranberry, and Woodsman's wild salal. Gift boxes for mailing are also available; call (503) 997–2252 for information. For other picnic foods and beverages, stop at the large market at the junction of Highway 101 and Highway 126 before leaving town.

Next turn off Highway 101 at the **Darlingtonia Wayside** sign, pull into the visitor parking area, and follow the shaded trail to the boardwalk that takes you out onto a marshy bog. This is one of the few small nature preserves in the United States set aside for conserving a single native species, *Darlingtonia californica,* often called cobra lily, because it captures and digests insects, or pitcher plant, because of its shape. You can see the unusual greenish-speckled plants here from spring through summer and into early fall.

Your next stop is **Devil's Elbow State Park,** just beyond Cape Creek Bridge, where you can walk the forested trail over to **Heceta Lighthouse** and its residence, the latter now used for meetings and retreats. The park's sheltered beach offers a lovely spot to picnic and to beachcomb for shells and driftwood. Offshore, the large rock "islands," part of the Oregon Islands National Wildlife Refuge, are transient nesting grounds for tufted puffin, cormorants, pigeon guillemots, and numerous kinds of seagulls.

By now, midway on your coastal trek, you have surely felt the magic of the ocean seeping into your civilized, though perhaps weary, bones. Emanating from the rhythmic tides and from the sound of the surf is a calmness that erases stress and causes one to relax into nature's cycles for a time. Even words like *magnificent, incredible,* and *awesome* seem inadequate to describe the wide-angle views along this stretch of the Oregon coast. It's a panoramic showstopper of the first order, and nearly every inch of it is open to the public.

For another spectacular view drive up to **Cape Perpetua** and its Visitors' Center, just a short distance off Highway 101, perched atop a jagged chunk of 40-million-year-old volcanic basalt. The Forest Service staff offer lots to see and do at Cape Perpetua, including six nature trails, camp-fire talks at Tillicum Beach, and naturalist-led hikes down to the tide pools, together with interpretive exhibits and films on marine fish, animal life, and plant life. The visitors' center is open all summer, every day, from 9:00 A.M. to 6:00 P.M.; call (503) 547–3289 for more information. Also within the area are group picnic areas, a campground, and a 22-mile self-guided auto tour.

For a pleasant bed-and-breakfast experience on the central coast, call Mary Lou Cavendish or Irv Tebor and reserve a room at the **Ziggurat Bed and Breakfast,** 95330 Highway 101, Yachats 97498 (503–547–3925). It's located about 6 miles south of Yachats and commands an oceanside setting and easy access to walking on the beach. Designed by the couple, the place makes you feel as though you're walking into a gigantic pyramid filled with windows and light. Comfortable sitting places offer peeks at the ocean.

Choose from the large, airy, ground-level suite, with its comfortable common area, from two large suites on the main floor, or from a nest that offers ocean views from its location high in the rafters on the fourth level. Irv bakes wonderful breads, and Mary Lou serves a delicious gourmet breakfast in the glass-enclosed sun room—if, that is, you can pull your relaxed body from beneath the comforter of your queen-size bed.

Detour from Highway 101 at Waldport and meander 9½ miles east on Highway 34 to enjoy breakfast, lunch, or dinner at **Kozy Kove Kafe.** Cammie and Bill Johns operate their floating restaurant on the Alsea River at Tidewater. As you sit in comfortable deck chairs, you'll often see small boats putter by and fat ducks waddle along the deck and plop into the water. During your meal you might spy harbor seals that have swum into the river from the ocean on the tide and, along the riverbank, wild goats and grazing deer and elk. Try the amazing burritos, the chicken or shrimp fajitas, or the fresh seafood. Summer hours are Tuesday through Sunday, 9:00 A.M.–8:00 P.M.; winter hours are Thursday–Friday, 11:00 A.M.–7:00 P.M., and Saturday–Sunday, 9:00 A.M.–8:00 P.M. For reservations call (503) 528–3251. At Tidewater turn at the grocery/RV park/marina; park and walk down the ramp; you won't see the "kafe" from the highway because it floats below the bank.

Continuing north again on Highway 101 for about 20 miles, the **Yaquina Bay Lighthouse** in Yaquina Bay State Park, near Newport, is open to visitors every day from noon to 5:00 P.M. from Memorial Day through Labor Day and on weekends during the rest of the year. Admission is 50 cents, with children under six admitted free. For tours arranged in groups of ten or more, call the South Beach State Park business office at (503) 867–7451.

To immerse yourself in central coast history, plan to stop at the **Burrows House Museum** and the **◆Log Cabin Museum,** both cared for by the Lincoln County Historical Society, at 545 SW Ninth Street in Newport. The Burrows House was built in 1895 by John and Susan Burrows at a cost of $1,400; the large house, including a tall cupola, was moved to its present location in 1976. Enjoy exhibits of pioneer furnishings and clothing, as well as photographs and other items depicting the history of Lincoln County. In the nearby Log Cabin Museum, you can see a collection of household artifacts from the Siletz Indian Reservation, along with logging, coastal-farming, and maritime exhibits. Both museums are open June through September from 10:00 A.M. to 5:00 P.M. daily and October through May from 11:00 A.M. to 4:00 P.M. each day but Monday. Call (503) 265–7509 for more information.

If you'd rather head into the hinterlands on your own, pick up a copy of the historical society's brochure *Historical Map of Lincoln County,* which offers a numbered map, explanations, and the locations of thirty-four historic sights and sites ranging from Cape Perpetua north to Lincoln City.

Before leaving the Newport area, you can refill your picnic basket or cooler from the carry-out section at **Canyon Way Restaurant,** which features homemade pastas, delicious breads, meat- or seafood-filled croissants, and pastries that include chocolate creations and delicious tortes. Located at 1216 SW Canyon Way, just a half-block up from the bay-front area, the restaurant is open Monday through Saturday from 11:00 A.M. to 3:00 P.M. The companion deli and bookstore are open from 10:00 A.M. to 8:30 P.M. Tuesday through Saturday.

Another historic structure in Newport, this one located in the historic Nye Beach area, is the renovated **◆Sylvia Beach Hotel,** at 267 NW Cliff Street. The building dates to 1910, was saved from the wrecker's ball by Sally Ford and Goodrun Cable, and is dedicated to the memory of Sylvia Beach, owner of the Shakespeare

Yaquina Bay Lighthouse

and Company Bookstore in Paris during the 1920s and 1930s and one of the twentieth century's great patrons of literature.

Each of the twenty guest rooms is furnished and decorated to reflect a different well-known author. The most elegant room, commemorating Agatha Christie, features English chintzes and ruffles, a tiled fireplace, and a deck overlooking the ocean—along with clues from her mystery novels strewn about. For dinner reservations and information about guest rooms, call (503) 265–5428. *Note:* The hotel is not suitable for children, and the rooms are without phones, television sets, or radios. Guests are invited to browse in the hotel's library on the third floor.

The Newport Visitors' Information Center offers travelers a toll-free number for obtaining current information about the variety of goings-on in the Yaquina Bay area; call (800) 262–7844.

Heading north again on Highway 101, you can access an optional scenic loop along the sea cliff, **Otter Crest Scenic Loop Drive,** at Otter Rock. First drive out to the bluff to peer down into **Devil's Punch Bowl,** a rounded outcropping into which the ocean thunders foamy waves: an especially dramatic display during winter storms, as well as on the incoming tide. The loop drive reconnects with Highway 101 within a couple of miles.

If you're driving through the area at low tide—you can pick up current tide tables for a nominal cost at most visitors' centers—stop at the **Inn at Otter Crest,** parking close to the ocean, just beyond the Flying Dutchman Restaurant. Walk a short path down to the beach, where you can see a fascinating array of **tide pools** formed by rounded depressions in the large volcanic rocks. Bathed by tidal currents twice each day, coastal tide pools may house a variety of species such as sea anenomes, sea urchins, goose barnacles, sea stars, sea slugs, limpets, jellyfish, and tiny crab.

Just a few precautions, however, from the naturalists: Seaweed is slippery, so you should avoid jumping from rock to rock; know exactly when low tide is and keep an eye on the incoming tide; watch for large "sneaker" waves that can appear out of the regular wave pattern; stay away from rolling logs, which can move quickly onto an unsuspecting tide-pooler, particularly a small child; don't remove marine creatures from the tide pools or take any live specimens with you.

Although the live marine creatures are always to be left undisturbed in their tide pools, combing Oregon's driftwood-strewn beaches can yield other treasures, ones that *can* be taken home, such as limpet and barnacle shells, sand-dollar shells, Japanese glass floats, dried kelp, driftwood, beach rocks, and translucent agates. Especially good beaches for finding agates, jaspers, coral, sea fossils, and ribbon stones can be discovered at Bandon, Whiskey Run, Agate Beach, and Cape Meares.

If your picnic basket and cooler are full of goodies and cold beverages, consider a lunch stop at one of the most charming coastal day parks, **Fogarty Creek Wayside,** just north of Depoe Bay and Pirate's Cove. Here you can walk a path that meanders through the park, alongside a small creek, and under the highway to a small sandy cove right on the edge of the ocean. Weather permitting, you can have your picnic with seagulls and sandpipers for company. In the park are picnic tables and rest rooms. It's a great place for families with small children.

If, however, you're driving through this section of the central coast early in the day and the ocean is flat and shimmering in the morning sun, consider stopping at the seawall in **Depoe Bay,** just south of Fogarty Creek, to see whether the gray whales are swimming past. Of the seven different kinds of whales plying the Pacific Ocean, the grays maneuver closest to the shoreline. Some 15,000 of the mammoth creatures migrate south from November to January and return north from March to May. This 12,000-mile round-trip is the longest known for any mammal. The whalers of the 1800s nearly wiped out the whale population, but in 1936 an international treaty was enacted to protect the enormous mammals.

The early morning hours are the best times to spot whale "blows"—water or condensation blown up to 12 feet above the water surface when the gentle giants exhale—before offshore winds create whitecaps and before the midafternoon sun casts a glare on the water. Equipment for **whale watching** is minimal—helpful are good binoculars, a camera and tripod, and warm clothing. Or just shade your eyes and squint, gazing west toward the horizon. You might be rewarded for your patience by seeing one of the grays "breach," that is, leap high out of the water and then fall back with a spectacular splash.

During one week in January and another week in March, about 160 volunteers at whale-watching sites all along the coast offer helpful information, brochures, maps, and assistance with spotting the gray whales. Look for the familiar logo WHALE WATCHING SPOKEN HERE and for the volunteers, ranging from school kids to oldsters, whose efforts are coordinated by the staff at the **Hatfield Marine Science Center** in Newport.

At both Shore Acres, located west of Coos Bay–North Bend, and at Cape Perpetua, north of Florence, you can view from glassed-in areas and stay dry to boot. Additional information and a current schedule can be obtained from the oceanographers and volunteers at Oregon State University Extension/Sea Grant, Hatfield Marine Science Center, in Newport; the phone number is (503) 867–3011.

In Gleneden Beach, tucked into the woods like Hansel and Gretel's cottage, **Chez Jeanette** offers one of the most romantic dining settings on the central coast. Fresh bread and marvelous desserts are baked every day, and the house specialties of fresh seafood, veal, and game are served with several different vegetables and two kinds of fruit. The tiny restaurant is located ½ mile south of Salishan Lodge on the Gleneden Beach Loop, 7150 Old Highway 101. Open daily for dinner from 5:30 to 9:00 P.M.; call (503) 764–3434 for reservations.

Following all this whale-spying and gourmet eating, stop by the **Catch the Wind Kite Shop** in Lincoln City for a look at kites of all sizes, shapes, colors, and prices. It's located just across the highway from the D River Wayside beach , where, on a particularly windy day, you can watch some of the spectacular and brightly colored kites being flown by kids of all ages. There are wheelchair-accessible rest rooms here and a visitors' information booth as well.

Actually, Lincoln City has been a favorite spot for honeymooning couples for a century and a half. Traveling by horseback on the Old Elk Trail along the Salmon River, missionary Jason Lee brought his bride, Anna Marie Pittman, together with Cyrus Shepard and *his* bride—and a guide, Joe Gervais. The two couples set up camp at nearby Oceanlake and evangelized the Salmon River Indians. The Jason Lee Campsite can be seen at Oceanlake, at the north end of Lincoln City, near Devil's Lake.

For helpful information about the entire Lincoln City area, stop at the visitors' center at the far north end of town, at 801 SW Highway 101 (503–994–3070).

ON LEWIS AND CLARK'S TRAIL

Leaving the bustling Lincoln City area, travelers notice a quieter, more pastoral ambience along Highway 101, which winds north from Otis toward Neskowin, Sandlake, Cape Lookout, Netarts, and Tillamook. Travel through this region in the early spring, when you'll see dairy cows munching lush green grass inside white-fenced fields, clumps of skunk cabbage blooming in bright yellows, and old apple trees bursting with pale pink blossoms on gnarled limbs.

Notice the native Oregon grape along the roadside, with tight clusters of bright yellow blooms; the low-lying salal, with its bell-shaped delicate pink flowers carpeting forested areas; and the gangly salmonberry bushes, showing pale white blossoms. On a coastal trek this is clearly the time to slow the pace and enjoy a kaleidoscope of springtime colors.

If you decide to head back to Portland and environs via Highway 18 from the Lincoln City area, consider waiting to eat until you reach **Eyvette's Brookside Cafe**. It's located on the highway 16 miles east of Otis Junction and near the community of Grand Ronde. With its red roof, walls of unpainted rough-sawn Douglas fir, open rafter ceilings, unpainted concrete floor, assorted wooden tables and chairs, and wood-burning stove, the place is comfortable and rustic. You'll notice cast-iron pans, weathered farm tools, and horse tackle on the walls and hanging from the rafters. Hungry travelers choose from seventy-four varieties of omelets and thirty-two breakfast specialties; twenty-three different kinds of sandwiches and nineteen different burgers; and, then, homemade desserts, breads, cinnamon and pecan rolls. Notice, too, the jars of homemade conserves, marmalades, and spreads—everything from blackberry and raspberry to apricot and kiwi—arranged on shelves along one wall. The cafe is open every day from 7:00 A.M. to 3:00 P.M.

Heading north on Highway 101 detour onto **Three Capes Scenic Drive,** heading toward Pacific City—which is really a village rather than a city—so that you can watch the launching of the **Dory Fleet,** one of the coast's most unusual fishing fleets. In the shadow of **Cape Kiwanda,** a towering sandstone headland, salmon-fishers from the Pacific City area launch flat-bottomed dories from the sandy beach into the protected waters near the large, offshore rock islands where those ever-present sea birds congregate.

You could also arrive in the late afternoon to see the dories return with the day's catch, skimming across the water and right onto the beach. The boats are then loaded onto large trailers for the night. If you're hungry, stop at **Grateful Bread Bakery** (34805 Brooten Road; 503–965–7337) for scrumptious baked goods and some of the coast's best breads as well as good sandwiches, take-out service, and an outside deck. For information about the dory fleet and about dory fishing trips, contact the Pacific City–Woods Visitors' Information Center, P.O. Box 331, Pacific City 97135 (503–965–6161).

For a comfortable overnight stop well off the beaten path, consider **Sandlake Country Inn,** located a few miles north of Pacific City. Nestled away from the ocean in a green bower of rhododendron, old roses, and Douglas fir, the large farmhouse was built in 1894 out of huge timbers from a shipwreck. The home had been in the same family for some eighty years when Margo and Charles Underwood purchased and refurbished it several years ago as a bed-and-breakfast inn.

Three spacious guest rooms offer peaceful hideaways with quantities of quiet. The Rose Garden Room, on the main floor, is a retreat of wicker furnishings and French doors opening onto a rose garden. You'll sleep beneath a whimsical canopy and have your own private bath.

Enjoy meeting other guests in the cozy common area on the main floor, poking through the bookshelves for a novel, ambling about the grounds when the rhododendrons or roses are blooming, or taking a leisurely soak in the garden spa. Both Margo and Charles are gourmet cooks and provide mouth-watering breakfasts as well as afternoon refreshments for their guests; you can also arrange ahead for a romantic dinner or a picnic basket. For further information and reservations, contact the Underwoods at 8505 Galloway Road, Cloverdale 97112 (503–965–6745).

Just north of Sandlake, nature trails at **Cape Lookout** offer a close-up view of a typical coastal rain forest that includes such species as Sitka spruce, western hemlock, western red cedar, and red alder. A thick tangle of salal, box blueberry, salmonberry, sword fern, and Pacific wax myrtle covers the forest floor beyond the path.

Then dig out the binoculars and stop far off the beaten path, at the tiny community of Oceanside, to walk on the beach and see **Three Arch Rocks.** These offshore islands were set aside in 1907 by President Theodore Roosevelt as the first wildlife preserve on the Pacific Coast. Carpeted with sea grass and yellow-flowering sulphurweed, the large rocks are home to thousands of black petrels, colorful tufted puffins, and penguinlike murres, along with several varieties of gulls and cormorants. The bellow of resident Stellar sea lions and sea pups can often be heard as well. *Note:* Rest-room facilities are located near the public parking area. There are small eateries here and overnight accommodations, some overlooking the ocean. For specific information contact the Tillamook Visitors' Center, (503) 842–7525.

From Oceanside continue north to the third cape, Cape Meares, which lies about 10 miles northwest of the thriving dairy community of Tillamook. Stop to visit the **Cape Meares Lighthouse** and also walk the short trail to see the **Octopus Tree,** an unusual Sitka spruce with six trunks. Bordering the paved path to the lighthouse are thick tangles of ruby rugosa roses with large burgundy blossoms; they're especially suited to salt air and coastal mists. You may well see folks sketching or photographing the picturesque circa 1890s structure that was deactivated in 1963. A photomural display is open daily during summer months, with friendly volunteers on hand to provide historic tales about the lighthouse. You can also learn about Tillamook County's history at the incredibly well-stocked **Pioneer Museum** located in the old Courthouse building at 2106 Second Street in Tillamook. You'll see the stagecoach that carried mail in the county's early days, several vintage horseless carriages, logging memorabilia along with stuffed animals and birds, the replica of a fire lookout, and a kitchen of yesteryear. The museum is a delight for all ages to visit. Hours are Monday–Saturday, 8:30 A.M.–5:00 P.M., and Sundays noon–5:00 P.M. (closed Mondays during winter months). For further information contact the museum staff at (503) 842–4553.

Linger awhile longer on this less populated section of the coast to visit the world's largest clear-span wooden structure, the ◆**World War II Blimp Hangar Museum,** and its collection of historic photographs, memorabilia, and vintage airplanes. The building, more than twenty stories high and ⅕ mile long, was the site of

Tillamook's Naval Air Station from 1942 to 1948. During the war it was essentially a blimp site. Avid airplane buffs are restoring some thirteen aircraft, such as a Chance-Vought F4U Corsair; a 1942 Stinson V-77 Reliant; a modified 1953 Boeing Stratocruiser called *The Guppy*; a Consolidated PBY-5A Catalina flying boat called *The Duck*; and one of the famous Spitfires that helped win the Battle of Britain. You can watch the restoration process and enjoy a short scenic flight in the Reliant biplane. Operated by the Port of Tillamook Bay, the museum is open daily 9:00 A.M.–6:00 P.M. from May to October and is open until 5:00 P.M. the remainder of the year (except major holidays). It's located 2 miles south of Tillamook, just off Highway 101, at 4000 Blimp Road. Needless to say, you can't miss spotting it! The telephone number is (503) 842–1130.

You could backtrack just a few miles more, about 7 miles south of Tillamook via Highway 101, to see the spectacular 266-foot **Munson Creek Falls**; it ranks as the highest waterfall in the Coast Range. The sign off Highway 101 directs you to a 1½-mile county road that leads to the parking area and trails. Take the lower trail, a short walk to the base of the falls and, if time allows, have your basket lunch there in the nearby picnic area. *Note:* There are no rest-room facilities here. For more information about waterfalls in the Coast Range and campgrounds in the area, contact the regional Oregon State Parks office at 13000 Whiskey Creek Road West, Tillamook 97141 (503–842–4981).

Just a mile north of Tillamook, in a converted dairy barn, the ◆**Blue Heron French Cheese Factory** produces delicious French-style Brie and Camembert cheeses. You can sample not only the cheeses but a good selection of Oregon wines and can purchase other international cheeses and deli foods. The tasting room and deli are located at 2001 Blue Heron Drive, just off Highway 101; the phone number is (503) 842–8281. The establishment is open daily from 8:00 A.M. to 8:00 P.M. during summer and from 9:00 A.M. to 5:00 P.M. during winter.

If you're itching to do a bit of shopping for coastal antiques, stop first in the tiny hamlet of Wheeler and find **Laknes's Pieffenschneider Antique Mall** just across from the train depot. It's filled with an eclectic mix of vintage furniture and small collectibles. For further information contact Lorraine Laknes at (503) 368–5197.

Highway 101 soon skirts Nehalem Bay and wends through the historic fishing village of Nehalem, known for crabbing and clamming and for fine fishing. Angling for silver and chinook salmon, cutthroat, native trout, and steelhead is among the best along the Nehalem River and bay area; there's a marina here with both free boat launches and private moorages. Canoe races are held on the river each spring.

For a second antiques shopping foray, trundle into **Nehalem Antique Mall,** where you can browse among an array of antique oak furniture, old books, excellent glassware, and a plethora of intriguing collectibles offered by fifty aficionados of vintage stuff, active dealers who rent space from the mall's enthusiastic owner, Carolyn Crowe. You can also pick up a free copy of *Old Stuff,* a voluminous tabloid that contains maps and information about antiques-hunting all over Oregon and the Northwest. For further information about the area—including fishing and crabbing, bicycle and horse trails, and annual festivals—contact the Nehalem Bay Area Visitors' Center, P.O. Box 238, Wheeler 97147 (503–368–5100).

Highway 101 now winds high atop Neahkahnie Mountain and then proceeds down to one of the north coast's most hidden coves and beach areas, ◆**Short Sand Beach** and **Oswald West Park.** If you seek a truly remote camping experience, try one of the thirty-six primitive campsites at Oswald West. Alternatively, have your beachside picnic at one of the many picnic spots at Short Sand Beach.

Here you can do what the early Native American families did—explore the agate- and driftwood-strewn cove, snoop into shallow caves and caverns, fish or wade in an icy creek or shallow streams, peer at delicate tide pools housed in large rock depressions, and let the sounds of the surf lull you to sleep on a blanket or, better yet, in a tent with the moon and stars casting shimmering bands of light across the water.

The particulars: Park in the large parking area along Highway 101 and walk the ½-mile trail to the beach, through old-growth Douglas fir, coast pines, salal, salmonberry, and ferns growing in lush profusion along the way. Wheelbarrows are available at the parking area for hauling in camping gear; the primitive campsites are reached by a ¼-mile trail from the picnic area. A section of the **Oregon Coast Hiking Trail** passes through the area as well. This remote beach area is accessible only by foot, a fact that tends to keep the crowds away, and it is not wheelchair-accessible. For further information contact the State Parks Office in Portland, 3554 SE Eighty-second Avenue, Portland 97266 (503–238–7488).

Sleeping in a tent on the sand is not your thing? Well, not to worry, there's a new forty-six room hostelry on the beach, ◆**Stephanie Inn,** located at Cannon Beach, just a few miles north via Highway 101. With your private deck, gas fireplace, VCR, terry-cloth robes, whirlpool tub, and evening turn-down service, and, after a marvelous night's rest lulled by soothing ocean sounds, when you awake to the delicious smells of fresh-brewed coffee and freshly baked breakfast breads, you'll wonder how a traveler could ask for more comfortable or civilized accommodations. Later, pull on tennis shoes and warm windbreakers for a walk on the beach north to **Haystack Rock,** the north coast's venerable landmark that houses colonies of sea birds and myriad tide pools. Then you could browse through Cannon Beach's main street art galleries, boutiques, and bookshops, or sip hot coffee and enjoy clam chowder at cozy cafes like **Dooger's** or **The Bistro** (also on Hemlock Street) before walking back to the inn for friendly conversation and complimentary wine served near the river-rock fireplace in the cozy main lounge. Many folks also like to retreat to the library and chart room to read, relax, and watch the ever-changing ocean and glorious sunsets from wide windows facing west. For supper the inn's chef offers two prix fixe northwest entrées (reservations recommended). For further information call Stephanie Inn's toll-free number, (800) 633–3466, or (503) 436–2221. The inn's address is P.O. Box 219, Cannon Beach 97110.

At the north edge of Cannon Beach, access and drive the shaded winding road up to **Ecola State Park** for one of the most dramatic seascape panoramas on the north coast. In the lush 1,300-acre park, you'll see splendid examples of old-growth Sitka spruce, western hemlock forest, native shrubs, and wildflower species. Deer and elk often browse nearby, and picnic tables are tucked here and there, many sheltered from coastal breezes. The views are spectacular, particularly on blue-sky days; walk the trails along the ledges and remain safely behind the fenced areas. You can spy migrating whales during winter months and ask questions of whale-watching volunteers stationed on the bluff during the latter part of March. *Note:* There are rest-room facilities here. Further information about the area can be obtained from the Cannon Beach Visitors' Center located at Second and Spruce streets, P.O. Box 64, Cannon Beach 97110. The telephone number is (503) 436–2623.

For those who want to plan hikes along the **Oregon Coast Trail,** some of which passes through scenic Ecola State Park and **Indian Beach,** maps and current information can be obtained from the State Parks and Recreation Division, 1115 Commercial Street NE, Salem 97310. The telephone number is (503) 378–6378.

Follow Highway 101 north to one of Oregon's oldest resort towns, Seaside, where families have vacationed since the turn of the century. For a nostalgic experience park the car on any side street near the ocean and walk as far as you like on the ◆ **Historic Seaside Promenade**—a 2-mile-long sidewalk, with its old-fashioned railing restored, that skirts the wide sandy beach. Benches are available here and there for sitting, and about the only discordant note in this pleasant reminiscence—folks have walked "the Prom" since the early 1900s—may be an occasional bevy of youngsters sailing by on roller skates.

The Lewis and Clark expedition reached the Pacific Ocean in 1804, near the Seaside area, and you can see the original salt cairn—just off the south section of the Prom on Lewis and Clark Avenue—where the company boiled seawater to make salt during the rainy winter of 1805.

Standing regally on the corner of Beach Drive and Avenue A is one of Seaside's historic homes, circa 1890, now the elegant ◆ **Gilbert Inn Bed and Breakfast.** Owners Carole and Dick Rees transformed the old dowager into a bed-and-breakfast inn and offer travelers ten spacious guest suites. In the Turrett Room on the second floor, you can sleep in a queen-size four-poster amid romantic, country French–style decor.

One can imagine that those circa 1837 honeymooners, Lees and the Shepards, would easily have exchanged their campsite on the beach near Lincoln City for these splendid accommodations. Carole serves a marvelous breakfast that includes such delights as layered French toast with warm apricot sauce, along with the usual—gourmet coffee, teas, freshly squeezed juices, and fresh fruit. For reservations contact the innkeepers at 341 Beach Drive, Seaside 97138 (503–738–9770).

For a close-up look at Lewis and Clark's 1804–06 winter headquarters, visit ◆ **Fort Clatsop National Monument,** about

10 miles north of Seaside, near Astoria. Walk the winding path from the interpretive center to the log replica of the encampment. Here, from June to September, you can see a living-history program that includes buckskin-clad park rangers, live musket firing, boat carving, tanning, and map making—all frontier skills used by the company during that first, extremely rainy winter.

Within 25 miles are several sites described in the Lewis and Clark journals. The Fort Clatsop brochure, available at the visitors' center, gives all the details and a helpful map.

Additional information about Fort Clatsop and about the annual summertime Lewis and Clark historical drama, *Journey to the Pacific,* can be obtained form the well-stocked Seaside Visitors' Information Center, 7 North Roosevelt Street, Seaside 97138 (503–738–6391).

Not far from the Lewis and Clark encampment, enterprising John Jacob Astor founded Astoria—just six years later, in 1811. Settled for the purpose of fur trading, the bustling seaport at the mouth of the Columbia River grew into a respectable city during the late 1800s. You can take a walking or a driving tour and see some of the 400 historic structures still remaining, including the historic **Astor Column** high atop Coxcomb Hill, the **Flavel Mansion Museum,** and many restored Victorian homes, many now open as comfortable bed-and-breakfast inns.

Built in 1883 by Captain George Flavel, the **Flavel Mansion,** now the **Clatsop County Historical Museum,** is one of the finest examples of Victorian architecture in the state. Located on Eighth Street, between Exchange and Duane streets, this impressive structure, with its columned porches, carved gingerbread detailing, and tall cupola, is worth a visit. The mansion is open daily from 10:00 A.M. to 5:00 P.M. during the summer and from noon to 5:00 P.M. during the winter, except Monday; phone (503) 325–2203 for more information.

Fort Astoria, on Exchange Street, is a partially restored fort, originally built by Astor's Pacific Fur Company in 1811. Nearby is the site of the first U.S. post office west of the Rocky Mountains, established in 1847. For a copy of *An Explorer's Guide to Historic Astoria,* contact the Astoria Visitors' Information Center, 111 West Marine Drive (P.O. Box 176-E), Astoria 97103 (503–325–6311).

Historic Astor Column

If you travel along the north coast during winter and early spring, stop and visit the **Twilight Eagle Sanctuary,** located just 8 miles east of Astoria, and ½ mile north of Highway 30 on Burnside Road. The protected area offers prime feeding and roosting for about forty-eight eagles. You can identify the noble birds by their white heads and tails, large beaks, and yellow legs. Then, too, during all four seasons, bird lovers far and wide find one of the best places on the coast to watch an enormous variety of bird species from the viewing platform at **Fort Stevens State Park,** located 10 miles west of Astoria near Hammond. Be sure to take along your binoculars or cameras with telephoto lenses. Call the Oregon Parks office in Portland (503–238–7488) to make campground reservations (a must during busy summer months).

SOUTHERN OREGON

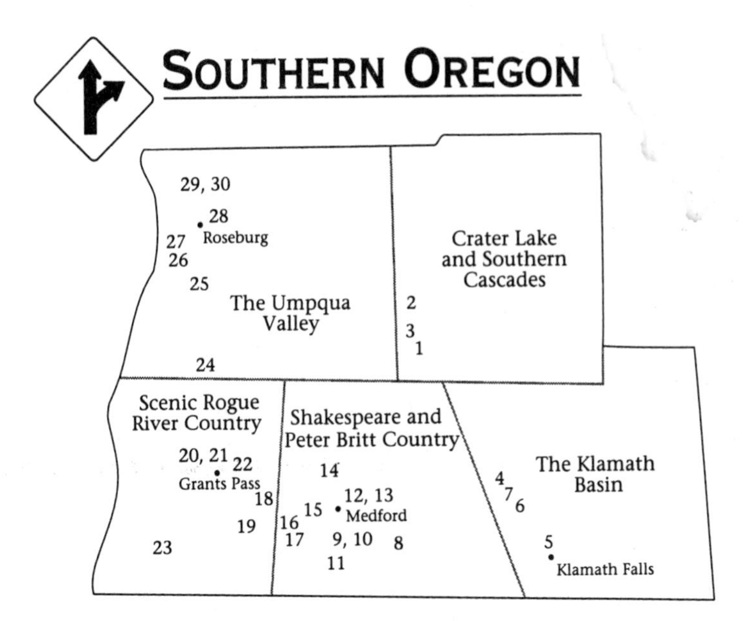

1. Crater Lake Rim Drive
2. Diamond Lake Resort
3. Pacific Crest National Scenic Trail
4. Klamath Basin National Wildlife Refuge
5. Baldwin Hotel Museum
6. Upper Klamath Canoe Trail
7. Sun Pass Ranch
8. Pinehurst Inn at Jenny Creek
9. Oregon Shakespearean Festival
10. Lithia Park and Japanese Garden
11. Mt. Ashland Inn
12. Railroad Park
13. Bear Creek Nature and Bicycling National Recreation Trail
14. Butte Creek Mill and Country Store
15. Under the Greenwood Tree Bed and Breakfast
16. Jacksonville Pioneer Cemetery
17. Peter Britt Music and Arts Festival
18. Willow Brook Bed and Breakfast
19. Wimer and McKee Covered Bridges
20. Rogue River
21. Pine Meadow Bed and Breakfast Inn
22. Wildlife Images Rehabilitation and Education Center
23. Oregon Caves National Monument
24. Wolf Creek Tavern
25. Sonka's Sheep Station Bed and Breakfast
26. Hillcrest Vineyard
27. Wildlife Safari
28. Douglas County Museum of History and Natural History
29. Oakland Historic District
30. Tolley's Restaurant and Antiques

SOUTHERN OREGON

CRATER LAKE AND SOUTHERN CASCADES

Southern Oregon is a curious mixture of old ghost towns and historic landmarks combined with white-water rivers, wildlife refuges, colorful caverns, a high-altitude volcanic lake, and national forests and mountain ranges containing some of the least-known wilderness areas in the Beaver State. In Oregon's only full-fledged national park, stunning **Crater Lake** shimmers like a crystal blue jewel in the enormous caldera of 12,000-foot Mt. Mazama. More than 6,000 years ago this peak in the southern Cascade Mountains collapsed with a fiery roar and formed a deep basin of 20 square miles; the lake is more than 1,500 feet deep in places.

The 33-mile-long **Crater Lake Rim Drive,** encircling the lake at an invigorating elevation of 6,177 feet, can be done in an hour or so, but to savor the 360-degree panorama and succession of splendid changing views, you'll want to plan a longer outing: Spend the whole day there, and then stay overnight in one of the several campgrounds in the area or in the venerable **Crater Lake Lodge** perched on the south rim.

You can also take a 6-mile side road from **Kerr Notch,** at the southeast corner of the rim, down to the Pinnacles, 200-foot spires of pumice and tuff (layers of volcanic ash). A 4-mile, one-way nature trail for motorists traverses Greyback Ridge, allowing a sit-down look at rock formations, native trees, and wildflowers. Within the park are some 85 miles of hiking and nature trails.

For another panoramic view take the two-hour boat trip from Crater Lake's 25-mile shoreline, accompanied by a Park Service interpreter. *Note:* The trail down to the dock is a very steep, 1.1-mile hike. Winter brings a sparkling snowy beauty to the lake, along with outdoor activities like cross-country skiing, snowshoeing, and ski touring. For information about winter tours—reservations are required—contact Crater Lake Ski Service, Crater Lake 97604 (503–594–2361).

A Portland mountain climber and transplanted Kansan, William Gladstone Steel, saw the lake in 1885 and helped lead the crusade to save the area around the park from homesteading.

He battled to have the area designated a national park, a measure approved by President Theodore Roosevelt on May 22, 1902, as the seventh such park to be established in the United States. The first horseless carriage motored up to the lake in 1905; by 1919 the spectacular Rim Drive, though just a bumpy dirt road, was a standard stop on sight-seeing rambles around the state.

William Steel was appointed the second superintendent of Crater Lake National Park in 1913, and the restored visitors' center, dating from 1934 and situated near the main headquarters building, is named in his honor. It's open throughout the year from 9:00 A.M. to 5:00 P.M. A smaller visitors' center, located between the lodge and the cafeteria–gift shop, is open during the summer season from 8:00 A.M. to 7:00 P.M. daily. Additional information can be obtained from staff at Crater Lake National Park, P.O. Box 7, Crater Lake 97604. Call (503) 594–2211 for park staff or (503) 594–2511 for campsites and cabins. Built in the early 1900s and opened in 1915, the historic lodge is currently undergoing complete renovation and will reopen in 1995. Accommodations will be available from June to early September.

Access the Crater Lake area via Highway 97 from Bend (about 80 miles); Highway 140 from Klamath Falls (about 60 miles); Highway 62 from Medford (about 70 miles); or Highway 138 from Roseburg (about 80 miles). This last entrance closes with the first heavy snowstorm, usually in mid-October, and reopens by mid-June or July; the south entrance remains open year-round.

Just north of Crater Lake National Park, at a lower elevation, is Diamond Lake, a smaller jewel nestled within Umpqua National Forest. Rainbow-trout season opens here the third weekend of April, and sailboats, motorboats, and canoes can be rented in advance. Moorage space is available throughout the summer and early fall, and fishing/hunting licenses can be purchased at the tackle shop.

Many campground sites, open from May through October, are found on the lakeshore; Diamond Lake and Broken Arrow Campgrounds have trailer dump stations. A well-stocked store is located near **Diamond Lake Resort.** Several lakeshore cabins are available as well—some with fireplaces and kitchens.

During winter take a guided snowmobile tour—ask about the special tour, including lunch, to Crater Lake—or arrange for snowcat skiing. Often space is available, but it's wise to call ahead for reservations. There's also a good "inner-tube" sledding hill for families with small children. During summer visitors enjoy horseback riding—special group rates can be arranged, and guides are also available. For further information about accommodations and winter or summer activities, write Diamond Lake Resort, Diamond Lake 97731 (503–793–3333).

Wilderness seekers, backpackers, and hikers can try climbing 8,363-foot Mt. Bailey—strenuous but worth the sweat—or the 4-mile trail to 9,182-foot Mt. Thielson. Both offer superb views of the southern Cascades, Crater Lake, and Diamond Lake. Rangers caution that summer is quite short at these alpine elevations; thus, be sure to dress adequately and to bring the proper gear, including sufficient food, water, and emergency shelter. For information about the **Pacific Crest National Scenic Trail,** which crosses the west side of the area and winds south through the wooded ridges and plateaus of Mountain Lakes Wilderness, contact the Diamond Lake Ranger Station (503–498–2531) near Toketee Falls or write the Regional Forester, P.O. Box 3623, Portland 97208.

Located 13 miles north of Diamond Lake, off Highway 138, Lemolo Lake offers one of the most peaceful outdoor camping retreats in the Umpqua National Forest. If you would rather not camp outdoors, you could stay overnight at tiny **Lemolo Lake Resort,** situated on the west side of the lake near Poole Creek Campground. To reserve one of the ten lodging units, contact the staff at HC 60, P.O. Box 79-B, Idleyld Park 97447, or call (503) 496–0900. Gasoline and food services are available here. In this quiet, forested spot, the loudest noises you hear may be gentle breezes that swish through the branches of tall Alpine fir or the friendly chatter of golden mantle squirrels, who often venture close enough to munch offerings of sunflower seeds and peanuts.

THE KLAMATH BASIN

Continuing your exploration of southern Oregon, head south via Highway 62 or 97 toward Klamath Falls to see another region of diversity, including one of the largest wildlife and wildfowl refuges in the Northwest. Many of the roads in this area, particularly Highway 66 from "K Falls" to Ashland, were used by early mail and freight stagecoach lines between the Klamath Basin and settlements along the Rogue River, to the west.

When it was the land of the ancient Ouxkanee, or "people of the marsh," the million-acre Klamath Basin contained a vast expanse of lakes and marshes ideal for waterfowl courtship and nesting. White settlers nearly drained the area dry for farmland, but beginning in 1908, in an effort aided by the emerging conservation ethic, portions of the Klamath Basin were set aside as wildlife refuges, secure from further encroachment. The last of the area reserved in 1958, the entire region is now known as the ◆ **Klamath Basin National Wildlife Refuge.** Though their domain is much smaller than in the days of the Ouxkanee, birds and waterfowl of all species crowd enthusiastically into what remains: some 83,000 acres of marsh and shallow lakes near Klamath Falls.

For the visitor, there are countless opportunities for close-up, nondisturbing viewing of waterfowl, marsh birds, shorebirds, and upland species—along lakes and marshes, near grassy meadows and farms, among the sagebrush and juniper, near ancient lava flows, and in nearby coniferous forests.

The great thrill is seeing the early spring or fall migrations, when the sky is dark with wings and the silence pierced by much cacophonous honking—climaxing to some 7 million birds en route along the **Pacific Flyway,** which extends the entire length of North and South America. First the ducks—pintails, ruddies, mallards, shovelers, and widgeons; then the geese—Canada, snow, white-fronted, and cackling . . . to mention just a few of the more than 270 species recorded here.

In March visitors can welcome the return of the white pelicans, Klamath Falls's feathery mascot; they nest and remain here until November. Link River and Lake Ewauna at **Veteran's Memorial Park** in Klamath Falls are among the most accessible places to see these large, curious birds, with their pouched beaks. And during winter some 500 bald eagles visit from the frozen North, attracting naturalists and bird lovers from all over to count and observe their nesting habits at an annual gathering the first week in January.

Information about viewing sites as well as helpful maps, including one for an auto tour, can be obtained from the Klamath County Visitors' Information Center, P.O. Box 1867, Klamath Falls 97601 (503–884–0666), or from the Klamath Basin Wildlife Refuge headquarters, Route 1, Box 74, Tulelake, CA 96134 (916–667–2231).

Klamath Falls, first named Linkville when founded in 1876, sits atop a geothermal area, and in early days many businesses and homes were heated by the hot water; the early native peoples used it for cooking.

The **Klamath County Museum,** at 1451 Main Street, offers exhibits and displays on the history, geology, anthropology, and wildlife of the Klamath Basin; it's open Tuesday through Saturday, 11:00 A.M. to 5:00 P.M. Also part of the museum complex, the four-story ◆**Baldwin Hotel Museum,** a noted turn-of-the-century hostelry built in 1906 by State Senator George Baldwin, offers a look at the hotel's opulent original furnishings and early history. Located at 31 Main Street, the brick building is open for tours from June to September, Tuesday through Saturday, 11:00 A.M. to 4:00 P.M.

Maud Baldwin, well-known photographer at the turn of the century, followed her father, George, around the county and into the marshes to record on film the area's early farmland reclamation project. More than 2,000 of her vintage photographs are housed at the **Klamath County Museum.** For further information call the museum complex staff at (503) 883–4208.

Many locals claim that the best place for lunch is **Saddle Rock Cafe,** where sandwiches, freshly baked pastries, desserts, and espresso can be ordered. Located at 1012 Main Street (503–884–1444), the cafe is open Sunday through Friday for breakfast and lunch, 7:30 A.M. to 2:00 P.M.; Friday and Saturday for dinner, 5:30 to 9:00 P.M.; and Sunday for brunch, 9:00 A.M. to 2:00 P.M. Then, too, you could swing into **Nibbley's Cream and Bean** for homemade ice cream or for gourmet coffees and teas along with freshly made soups and quiches. Located at 1831 Avalon, in the Shasta Plaza Mall, the cafe is open daily except Sundays. The telephone number is (503) 883–2314.

Just 30 miles north of Klamath Falls via Highway 97 is **Collier State Park and Logging Museum,** where you can take a gander at the largest collection of logging equipment in the United States. Be sure to look for the huge steam locomotive—it ran on roads rather than tracks. On your way to or from the park and museum, stop at the Ouxkanee Lookout for a panoramic view of Spring Creek Valley and for historical information about the region.

For a special outdoor experience, ask about the ◆**Upper Klamath Canoe Trail,** particularly the northern section where you can canoe gently along the 50-foot-wide trail and can often see families of beavers who live in the marshes; paddle close to the bulrushes to spy their connecting trails. A mother beaver will often slap her broad foot-long tail on the water to warn her family of your presence. For canoe and kayak rentals, contact **Rocky Point Resort,** 28121 Rocky Point Road, Klamath Falls, 97601 (503–356–2287). Take Highway 140 along the west side of Upper Klamath Lake about 28 miles and turn at the signs to the resort; the put-in spot is nearby.

If you decide to stay overnight in the area, check out the accommodations at Rocky Point or call Darlene Nimmo and Ron Rima, owner-innkeepers at **Sun Pass Ranch** located near Fort Klamath. Here, on a working ranch of one hundred acres near Wood River and Upper Klamath Lake, you can commune with llamas, goats, and turkeys as well as go canoeing or fishing. Guests explore hundreds of miles of nearby forest trails and backcountry roads, in the winter by clamping on cross-country skis, and, in the summer atop mountain bikes or on guided horseback rides (there are some nineteen horses at the ranch plus stables for boarding your own horse). If you prefer, you can hole up at the ranch and enjoy the animals, both wild and domestic; hundreds of bird species; and, distant purple mountain vistas such as Pelican Butte, Rustler Peak, and Saddle Mountain. Darlene serves a hearty ranch breakfast, often with warm apple muffins, sausage, and eggs. For dinner try the **Cattle Crossing Cafe** in Fort Klamath, open 6:00 A.M. to 10:00 P.M. For further information and reservations, contact Sun Pass Ranch, Highway 62 at the Wood River Bridge, P.O. Box 516, Fort Klamath (503–381–2259). Canoers can also find good floating and paddling on Crystal Creek and on Lake Ewauna in Klamath Falls.

For nearby campgrounds, hiking trails, places to fish, helpful maps, and general visitor information, stop by the Winema National Forest headquarters at 2819 Dahlia Street in Klamath Falls (503–883–6714), open Monday through Friday from 8:00 A.M. to 4:30 P.M.

By this time your senses will have become saturated with the wonder of Crater Lake's crystalline waters; the quietness and mystery of the southern Cascade Mountains wilderness areas will have seeped into your bones. Having experienced the breathtaking sight of a half-million or so ducks, geese, swans, white pelicans, and other waterfowl and wildlife congregating along the

Pacific Flyway near Klamath falls, you can now head further east, via Highway 395 or 140, into Oregon's Old West country; north on Highway 97, into Oregon's high desert country; or west on Highway 66, toward Ashland, Medford, and Jacksonville.

SHAKESPEARE AND PETER BRITT COUNTRY

Heading west on Highway 66 from Klamath Falls, stock up on groceries and consider holing up in one of the rustic cabins (all have kitchens) at **Green Springs Box R Ranch,** located along the historic Applegate Trail. Those weary pioneers who detoured from the Oregon Trail along this southern route in the mid-1840s often rested in this place at the 3,600-foot elevation level, near the springs and lush meadow. The ranch house, built in 1904, sits alongside the meadow, which in late spring and summer bursts with blooming wildflowers.

The ranch served originally as a stagecoach stop. Today it is a guest ranch and working cattle ranch of more than 1,000 acres, a place where you can help gather eggs from the henhouse, feed woolly spring lambs, or just relax and do nothing but soak in those marvelous southern Cascade Mountain sunrises and sunsets. You can also enjoy a sleigh ride during a winter visit or a wagon ride during the rest of the year, both activities involving a friendly pair of large Belgian horses, Willy and Waylon, harnessed and hitched and ready to go. A teamster-guide will share lively tales about the historic Applegate Trail as you tour a small pioneer village containing some of the oldest structures in southern Oregon.

For further information and reservations, write Box R Ranch, 16799 Highway 66, Ashland 97520 (503–482–1873). The ranch is located ½ mile off the highway, 39 miles west of Klamath Falls and 23 miles east of Ashland. There is also a 3,650-foot elevation airstrip nearby that can accommodate small planes; prior to use contact the FAA at (503) 378–4880.

Another option is to hole up in one of the five cozy bed-and-breakfast guest rooms at **◆Pinehurst Inn at Jenny Creek,** a handsomely restored, 1920-style roadhouse located just ¼ mile down the drive from the ranch house. Lunch and dinner are available in the inn's sunny dining room, on the main level; guests are served a full breakfast. Jenny Creek, well known for its brown trout fishing, bubbles alongside the inn, and you may even spy oddly shaped beaver lodges along its banks as well. For further information and reservations, contact the staff at Pinehurst Inn, 17250 Highway 66, Ashland 97520 (503–488–1002).

Highway 66 intersects with busy Interstate 5 near Ashland, just north of Mt. Ashland and the Siskiyou Pass, which takes travelers to and from the Oregon-California border. Detour at this intersection into the bustling community of Ashland, where you can take in a southern Oregon Shakespeare tradition that dates from 1935.

In that year young professor Angus Bowmer of Southern Oregon Normal School—later renamed Southern Oregon State College—conceived the idea of producing Shakespeare's plays by reworking the walls of the town's old Chautauqua Building into an outdoor theater reminiscent of those of Elizabethan England. Convincing Ashland's city leaders took some time, but with their conditional blessing the first productions—*Twelfth Night* and *The Merchant of Venice*—took place over the Fourth of July in 1935.

The deficits from a boxing match that was scheduled to satisfy the Shakespeare skeptics were covered by the resounding success and bulging receipts from the two plays. In 1937 the ◆**Oregon Shakespearean Festival** Association was organized as a nonprofit corporation, and in 1941 the first scholarships for actors were offered. The festival will celebrate its sixtieth year in 1995.

To complement the outdoor Elizabethan Theatre, the indoor Angus Bowmer Theatre was built in 1970 and the intimate Black Swan Theatre constructed in 1977. The three theaters anchor a large outdoor plaza, a gift shop, and ticket offices. The visitor can also poke into interesting shops and eateries along nearby Main Street.

For information about the current repertoire of traditional as well as contemporary offerings—eleven or more plays are staged from mid-February through October, ranging from *Hamlet, The Tempest,* and *Much Ado about Nothing* to *You Can't Take It With You, The Fifth of July,* and *The Rehearsal*—write the Oregon Shakespearean Festival, P.O. Box 158, Ashland 97520 or phone the box office at (503) 482–2111. *Note:* The plays staged at the outdoor Elizabethan Theatre run from June through October.

Be sure to ask for a complete schedule, including information about the Backstage Tour; the Exhibit Center, where you can try on a bevy of costumes, ranging from the garb of queens, kings, courtesans, and heroes to that of villains, monsters, madmen, and fools; and special festival events held throughout the nearly year-round season. A traditional, summertime feast officially opens the Shakespearean Festival season in mid-June. It's held, amid much music and colorful heraldry, in Ashland's lovely ◆**Lithia Park.**

For a quiet respite visit the park's exquisite ◆**Japanese Garden,** located on a gentle slope across from the Butler-Perozzi Fountain (access from the street that skirts the park's perimeter). You'll stroll graveled paths and giant stepping-stones, perhaps pausing to sit at one of several benches placed to catch the best views of native shrubs, many tree species, and a gently flowing stream.

Along with the plays of William Shakespeare, another English tradition is alive and well in Ashland. Many comfortable bed-and-breakfast inns offer such heartwarming amenities as goose-down comforters, wine or sherry by a crackling fire in the evening, and sumptuous continental or full breakfasts. You might have home-made peach preserves, piping-hot popovers or banana muffins, Dutch babies, and a special mushroom quiche, along with gourmet coffee and teas—all served on the best china, of course.

Because of the busy theater season, it's best to make lodging reservations early. For helpful brochures contact the Ashland Visitors' Information Center, P.O. Box 1360, Ashland 97520 (503–482–3486). When you stop by the visitors' center—located on Main Street near the Festival Center—ask about the self-guided walking tour brochure and map of historic buildings and homes, the *Inside and Outdoor Activities* guide, and winter sports information for nearby Mt. Ashland.

If the notion of sleeping in a 4,200-square-foot, handcrafted mountain log lodge sounds appealing, consider ◆**Mt. Ashland Inn,** just off the beaten path—about 16 miles south of town, on the road up to 7,528-foot Mt. Ashland. Owners Elaine and Jerry Shanafelt selected the logs from their own 160 acres of alpine wonderland at the 5,500-foot level. After cutting and stripping some 275 incense cedar logs, Jerry, an architect, coordinated the entire construction and then did all the plumbing, wiring, and finish work.

The results are stunning. Climb up log steps to a large deck and stop for a moment to savor the wide-angle view past tall pines to the verdant slopes of the Siskiyou mountain range, the valley floor, and 14,162-foot, snowy Mt. Shasta, looming some 50 miles to the south in northern California.

An enormous stone fireplace dominates the inviting common area, beckoning guests to the cheerful fire with a good book or a glass of hot spiced cider. The aroma of fresh-baked cookies may tempt a peek into the cozy kitchen just beyond the dining area. Choose from five comfortable guest rooms on the third level, each with a private bath. The Mt. McLoughlin king suite offers a homey sitting area and views to the east and south.

Antiques collected over many years, together with lovely patchwork quilts made by Elaine, furnish the rooms. Jerry's stained-glass windows and wood-carved archways and doors are seen throughout the inn as well. At breakfast a shrimp quiche or Normandy omelet, along with apple bundt cake, granola, orange juice, and biscuits with local honey and homemade preserves, provides a waist-expanding meal.

Work off the calories with an outdoor stroll or with a hike along a section of the **Pacific Crest Trail,** which crosses the inn's parking area. The trail angles through groves of ponderosa pine and red-barked manzanita up to lush alpine meadows that burst with colorful wildflowers in mid- to late summer. The wild larkspur, blue lupine, and white bear grass usually peak in August at the higher elevations.

During winter clamp on cross-country skis and enjoy a trek right from the inn's door, on the old logging roads located nearby—or try the snowshoes and sledding equipment kept handy for guests. To arrange a visit—the inn is open year-round—contact the Shanafelts at Mt. Ashland Inn, 550 Mt. Ashland Road (P.O. Box 944), Ashland 97520 (503–482–8707).

Right next door to Ashland is Medford, the Rogue River Valley's industrious timber-processing and pear-packing center. Once the home of the Takelma Indians, the region changed drastically when gold was discovered near Jacksonville, just west of Medford, in 1852. Miners invaded the valley in search of fortunes in gold nuggets and were followed by early settlers lured to the valley by its fertile soil and favorable growing conditions. The fortune hunters panned and claimed, the farmers cleared and planted—and both groups displaced the peace-loving Takelma tribe.

In 1883, when the Oregon and California Railroad reached southern Oregon, a railroad station was built at Middle Ford on Bear Creek—the community of Jacksonville apparently elected not to cough up the $25,000 "bonus" for the privilege. Later a town site was platted at Middle Ford and the name shortened to Medford. Incorporated in 1885, the town took up its first order of business: to establish an ordinance that discouraged disorderly conduct. A second ordinance prevented minors from loitering at the railroad depot, and a third solemnly prohibited hogs from running loose within the town.

To recapture some of the nostalgia and history connected with the railroad's reaching into the Rogue River Valley at Medford, visit ◆**Railroad Park,** where you can take a short train ride on the second and fourth Sundays of the month from 10:00 A.M. to 3:00 P.M. The historic park and its vintage train are located near Berrydale Avenue and Table Rock Road. For additional information contact the Medford Visitors' Information Center, at 304 S. Central, Medford 97501 (503–772–5194).

The **Southern Oregon Historical Society Center** also contains exhibits and historical collections and is a worthwhile addition to your travel itinerary. Recently relocated from Jacksonville, the center is located at 106 N. Central Avenue in downtown Medford (503–773–6536) and is open from 9:00 A.M. to 5:00 P.M. weekdays and from 10:00 A.M. to 5:00 P.M. Saturdays.

Medford is loved by bicyclists for its ◆**Bear Creek Nature and Bicycling National Recreation Trail,** which meanders through town along the banks of Bear Creek. Walkers and joggers are also welcome to use the paved trail. The Old Stage Road to Jacksonville, though heavily used by automobiles, is also popular with bicyclists. Bicycles can be rented at Siskiyou Cyclery, 1259 Siskiyou Boulevard; the visitors' information center will know of other resources as well.

Detour just 10 miles north of Medford on Highway 62 to visit the historic ◆**Butte Creek Mill** in Eagle Point. From the long wooden loading dock, step into the dim, coolish interior, where you can watch the miller at work. The tangy fragrance of wheat, rye, and corn will tantalize your nostrils, and you'll hear the faint bubbling sound of the creek, whose waters are turning two enormous millstones, 1,400 pounds each.

These giant stones were quarried in France; milled in Illinois; shipped around Cape Horn to Crescent City, on the northern California coast; and carried over the Coast Range mountains by wagon. They were first used for grinding grain here more than a hundred years ago. You can walk down to the lower level for a

Butte Creek Mill

peek at the myriad moving belts, shafts, and pulleys—water diverted from Butte Creek activates the turbine that turns the wheels, generating power for the mill; the spent water then reenters the stream through the tail race, located below the waterwheel.

The large wooden building has perched alongside Little Butte Creek since 1872 and was one of the first flour mills built in the Rogue River Valley. It's now the only remaining gristmill still in operation in Oregon. In addition to the freshly ground flours, meals, and cracked grains, you'll find old-fashioned peanut butter, nuts, dried fruits, seeds, granolas, yeasts, raw honey, molasses, teas, and bulk spices in the adjoining **Country Store.** A great place to take the kids as well, Butte Creek Mill and its old-fashioned Country Store is open year-round, Monday through Saturday from 9:00 A.M. to 6:00 P.M. There is a small museum next door, open by appointment. For further information call (503) 826–3531.

A pleasant option is to take the scenic route to the National Historic Landmark community of Jacksonville—the **Old Stage Road** off Highway 99 from the Central Point–Medford area—for a close-up view of tidy pear orchards, open-air fruit stands, and old farmsteads. During early spring the whole valley seems a canopy of luscious white pear blossoms. This eye-catching spectacle takes place from mid- to late April; call ahead to one of the visitors' information centers for current weather and bloom times.

Among the amenable bed-and-breakfast inns in the area is the historic **Under the Greenwood Tree Bed and Breakfast,** formerly a weigh station for hay and grain in the 1870s and 1880s. Situated comfortably amid enormous old oak trees and lush green lawns and gardens, the large square farmhouse was renovated by owner and world traveler Renate Ellam. Guests enjoy afternoon high tea served in the common area and are often treated to a personal tour of the grounds, including the old weigh-station scales, barns, vegetable and flower gardens, resident mules, and cages of twittering songbirds on a large deck overlooking the grounds.

Four lovely guest rooms, all with private baths, offer views from the second floor. Breakfast is a tempting gourmet affair, cooked fresh each morning and accompanied by steaming hot coffee and teas. For further information and reservations, contact Renate Ellam at Under the Greenwood Tree, 3045 Bellinger Lane, Medford 97501 (503–776–0000). The inn is about midway between Medford and Jacksonville.

Following the discovery of gold in the area in 1851, the Jacksonville community emerged in a matter of weeks. The fast-and-furious life of a gold rush town took over immediately. After the first wave of several thousand gold seekers came many wagon trains loaded with settlers and their families: the future solid citizens responsible for Jacksonville's transition to an agricultural community instead of a post–gold rush ghost town.

Designated a National Historic Landmark in 1966 by the U.S. Department of the Interior, the town of Jacksonville diligently works to preserve the atmosphere of the mid-1800s. Yet one can be just a mild history buff and still enjoy a visit—park on any side street and stroll down California Street for a glimpse into the colorful past.

The clump of miners' boots, the crunch of wagon wheels pulled by mules or horses, the laughter of the saloon and dance hall queens, and perhaps a gunshot or two seem to echo here and there—through rusted hinges, around the old iron town water pump next to the 1863 Beekman Bank Building, and around the circa 1891 railway depot now housing the Jacksonville Visitors' Information Center.

You can see a small length of the original track at the corner of Fifth and C streets. To savor an even closer feeling for Jacksonville's colorful history, trek from the old depot up E Street to the ♦**Jacksonville Pioneer Cemetery.** Situated on a small hill shaded by tall oak and madrone trees, the historic cemetery offers quiet paths into the past. Wax myrtle trails its heart-shaped leaves and small purple blossoms around vintage headstones, many of which date back to the early 1800s, and wildflowers like shooting stars and fawn lilies poke up here and there in shady nooks and crannies in early spring. Pick up a helpful map and six-page self-guided walking tour and history guide of the cemetery at the Visitors' Information Center. Don't miss this lovely spot.

The large white Courthouse Building, constructed in 1883 when the town housed the county seat—a vote to move the seat of county government to Medford was approved around 1926—is now the **Jackson County Historical Society Museum.** Plan a visit to this fine museum, with its historic collections of photographs, vintage clothing, books, and other pioneer memorabilia. Picnic tables are set on the grounds under tall, old- fashioned locust trees during summer months.

Living-history programs are offered during summer at **Beekman House,** located on California Street near the restored, circa 1854 Methodist church. Then stroll along the side streets to see more than eighty restored homes and other structures, many dating to the early 1800s, and all labeled; some have their own private gardens, which can be enjoyed from the sidewalk.

For information about other living-history exhibits and programs, contact the Jacksonville Visitors' Information Center, 185 N. Oregon Street (P.O. Box 33), Jacksonville 97530 (503–899–8118).

Other old buildings, now restored, house specialty shops and boutiques, ice-cream parlors, bakeries, and cafes. The 1863 **Jacksonville Inn** offers a good restaurant that is open for breakfast, lunch, and dinner (503–899–1900).

Walk up First Street to the Britt Gardens, founded in 1852 by pioneer photographer, horticulturist, and vintner Peter Britt. Named in his honor, the ◆**Peter Britt Music and Arts Festival** offers a wide variety of classical, bluegrass, jazz, and dance music, the events all taking place outdoors under the stars during June, July, and August. Collect a picnic, blankets, lap robes, pillows, or lawn chairs and find just the right spot on the wide lawn (or on wooden benches) for the evening's concert.

The festival has hosted such notables as Mel Tormé and Diane Schuur, Les Brown's band and the Dave Brubeck quartet, pianist Lorin Hollander, and dancers from the Royal Ballet Company of Covent Garden, London. At least four evenings are devoted to bluegrass concerts, and you can also enjoy a champagne brunch concert, the Rogue Valley Chorale and family concerts as well as participating in a wide variety of music and dance workshops.

For a helpful booklet listing the schedule and for ticket information, contact Britt Festivals, P.O. Box 1124, Medford 97501. After the first week of May, tickets can be purchased at the Britt Box Office at 46 North Front Street in Medford from 9:00 A.M. to 6:00 P.M.; call (503) 773–6077 or, for groups of ten or more, (503) 779–0847.

For overnight stays in the Jacksonville area, try **Old Stage Inn** (503–899–1776), a beautifully restored pioneer family house at the edge of town; **Reames House Bed & Breakfast** (503–899–1868), another vintage restoration in a garden setting on California Street; **Colonial House Bed & Breakfast** (503–770–2783), a restored Georgian country estate 1½ miles from town; or you could stay in nearby Medford at **Waverly Cottage Bed & Breakfast** (503–779–4716). Britt Festival–goers need to arrange reservations in February or March for the August gala to avoid being disappointed.

SCENIC ROGUE RIVER COUNTRY

If time allows, take winding old Highway 99 and Highway 199 for a leisurely, 25-mile drive along the upper Rogue River to Grants Pass. You can also detour at Gold Hill to visit the **Old Oregon Historical Museum,** located at 2345 Sardine Creek Road. Containing the largest private collection in southern Oregon, the museum is generally open daily from April to mid-October. If the notion of staying overnight in a charming, restored gold miner's farmhouse sounds intriguing, call former New Yorkers JoAnn and Tom Hoeber, now happily relocated as the owners and innkeepers of ◆**Willow Brook Bed and Breakfast,** 628 Foots Creek Road, Gold Hill 97525 (503–582–0075). Guests are welcome to use the swimming pool and hot tub. Tom has a wonderful herb garden and JoAnn spins local wools and knits colorful sweaters; ask about seeing the gentle Nubian goats, too.

If you love old covered bridges, plan to visit ◆**Wimer Covered Bridge,** the only one in Jackson County open to vehicle traffic. Originally constructed in 1892, the current covered structure, often called "a barn over water," was built in 1927 by Jason Hartman, a county bridge superintendent. To find the vintage covered bridge, detour from the town of Rogue River about 7 miles north on East Evans Creek Road; you may also see signs of a forest fire that raged through the area during early August 1992. For information on other covered bridges in the area, call the Southern Oregon Historical Society library in Medford, (503) 773–6536. In Rogue River you can visit **Palmerton Arboretum** and walk a 200-foot swinging footbridge, Skevington's Crossing, that crosses Evans Creek and connects the lovely five-acre arboretum with **Anna Classick City Park.**

For an alternate route from Jacksonville, take Highway 238, which winds gently along the Applegate River, passes the ◆**McKee Covered Bridge,** and turns north from Murphy into Grants Pass. Entering town via either route, you'll cross the Rogue River on the circa 1931 Caveman Bridge, which is on the National Register of Historic Places. For a list of other historic sites, write or stop by the well-stocked Grants Pass Visitors' Information Center, located at 1501 NE 6th Street, Grants Pass 97526 (503–476–7717).

The ◆**Rogue River** earns its nickname, "the fishingest river in the West," if you judge from the large number of folks who fish its pools and riffles year-round. The best chinook salmon

Rogue River

angling is reported to take place from mid-April through September, whereas summer trout fishing picks up in August and again in December through March. Local tackle shops sell bait, supplies, the required licenses, and salmon/trout tags. Ask about catch regulations.

You can fish from the shore at parks along the river or hire a drift-boat guide for half-days or full days—a tradition since the early 1930s, long before an 84-mile stretch of the river, on the south coast, between Grants Pass and Gold Beach, was designated part of the National Wild and Scenic System. More adventurous anglers can check out the three- and four-day guided fishing trips down this section of the Rogue that are offered by licensed outfitters from September 1 to November 15; the visitors' information center will have current information.

The most common summer white-water trips use large, inflatable oar-and-paddle rafts, inflatable kayaks, drift boats, or the popular jet boats. As you drift along with an expert guide handling the oars, the Rogue River ripples, cascades, boils, churns, and spills over rocks and boulders, through narrow canyons and gorges, and along quiet, pondlike, and peaceful stretches—rimmed on both sides by forests of Douglas fir, madrone, and oak and reflecting sunlight, blue sky, and puffy white clouds from its ever-moving surface.

You can also enjoy a one-day guided raft trip on the river or a four-hour, 36-mile jet-boat excursion to Hellgate Canyon, stopping at OK Corral for a country-style barbecue dinner served on a large deck overlooking all that marvelous river and wilderness scenery. Local kids love to entertain jet-boat passengers by swinging out over the river on long ropes attached to bankside trees, dropping and splashing—among much clapping and raucous laughter—into the river near lovely **Schroeder County Park and Campground,** just a few miles from downtown. For information and reservations contact Hellgate Jetboat Excursions, P.O. Box 982, Grants Pass 97526 (503–479–7204).

If you'd like to remain a little closer to civilization, consider spending the night at ◆**Pine Meadow Bed and Breakfast Inn.** Nestled in a pine forest with views of Mt. Walker and Mt. Sexton, guests immediately feel the stress-free, peaceful atmosphere created by innkeepers Nancy and Maloy Murdock. For starters you'll settle into a comfortable guest room decorated with early American antiques and offering sitting places like maple rocking chairs, comfy wing chairs, or a cozy window seat with pillows. Later, enjoy a leisurely soak in the outdoor hot tub, walk or ride bicycles on shady trails and country roads, and stroll hand in hand through the couple's lovely gardens. Breakfast is perhaps most memorable because it is healthy and light, yet gourmet. You might be served, for example, a fresh veggie egg bake, country potatoes, and Morning Glory muffins along with strawberries in sour cream and brown sugar. Almost everything is fresh from the vegetable and herb garden, and the juices served are organic. For further information and reservations, contact the Murdocks at 1000 Crow Road, Merlin 97532 or call them at (503) 471–6277. The inn is located just a few miles north of Grants Pass and the Rogue River, 6 miles from Interstate 5 via the Merlin-Galice Road.

Before heading north via Interstate 5 toward Roseburg, or going west via the Redwood Highway 199 toward Cave Junction and the coast, plan a natural history stop at **Wildlife Images Rehabilitation and Education Center.** Originally started to nurse injured birds of prey back to health, the center now aids and nurtures all types of injured or orphaned wild animals, from bears and fawns to raccoons and beaver. To arrange a guided tour, available at 11:00 A.M. and 1:00 P.M. daily, call ahead, (503) 576–0222. The center is located 13 miles from town; from G Street head west to Upper River Road, then onto Lower River Road.

For another scenic side trip, take the 20-mile paved, twisting road east of Cave Junction, located 50 miles west of Grants Pass via Highway 199, up to the **Oregon Caves National Monument.** Located in the heart of the Siskiyou Mountains at an elevation of 4,000 feet, the prehistoric marble and limestone underground caverns were discovered by Elijah H. Davidson in 1874, although native peoples, of course, knew about the caves for centuries before white people arrived.

Though guided walks through the caves can be taken year-round, you may want to avoid midsummer crowds and long lines by planning a trip in either early spring or late fall, after Labor Day. Better yet, try a midwinter visit in the snowy wonderland, bringing along your snowshoes or cross-country skis.

The cave tour, somewhat strenuous, lasts about seventy-five minutes and is not recommended for those with heart, breathing, or walking difficulties; canes and other walking aids are not permitted inside the caverns. And though children under six are prohibited from entering caves, a baby-sitting service is available for a nominal fee. *Note:* The caverns are a chilly 41 degrees Fahrenheit inside; dress warmly and wear sturdy shoes.

Also worth exploring are some of the nearby paths and hiking trails: 3-mile Big Tree Trail, through a virgin conifer forest; ¾-mile Cliff Nature Trail, offering wide vistas of the western Siskiyou Mountains; and 1.8-mile Caves Creek Trail following Cave Creek to the campground, where you'll find overnight camping facilities, a Forest Service ranger station, and informative campfire programs on summer evenings.

Then, too, you could stay the night at the rustic **Oregon Caves Chateau,** built in 1934 and now on the National Register of Historic Places. It's a handsome cedar structure with twenty-two guest rooms, some overlooking a waterfall and a pond, others the Douglas fir–clothed canyon or the entrance to the caverns. The chateau's restaurant serves dinner, offering steak, seafood, chicken, and a selection of Northwest wines, with Cave Creek close by—it bubbles right through the dining room. The coffee shop is open from 7:00 A.M. to 6:00 P.M. The Oregon Caves Chateau operates from mid-June to September; for more information, write the chateau at P.O. Box 128, Cave Junction 97523 (503–592–3400).

If you'd like to add a bottle of wine to your picnic basket or cooler, stop by **Siskiyou Vineyard's** winery and tasting room, where visitors are welcome to use the picnic area and to walk through the nature trails on the grounds. Located at 6220 Caves Highway (503–592–3727), about 6 miles from the junction of Highways 199 and 49, the vineyard is open daily from 11:00 A.M. to 5:00 P.M.

THE UMPQUA VALLEY

Early travelers came through southern Oregon by stagecoach over those rough, dusty, and sometimes muddy roads from central California on their way north to the Oregon country. The trip from San Francisco to Portland took about sixteen days, the fare being about 10 cents a mile. Stage stations were situated every 10 or so miles, and the big crimson-colored stages, built to carry the mail and as many as sixteen passengers, were an important link in the early development of the Northwest.

Completion of the railroad through the Willamette and Umpqua valleys south to California brought a sudden halt to the overland mail stage, thus marking the end of a colorful chapter in Northwest history; nevertheless, today's traveler can recapture a bit of that history. For a look at one of the oldest stage stops in the state, detour from Interstate 5 at Wolf Creek, about 20 miles north of Grants Pass. Here you will find historic ◆ **Wolf Creek Tavern**—dating from 1857—a large, two-story, Classic Revival–style inn that is still open to travelers.

Purchased by the state and completely restored in 1979, the inn is now administered by the State Parks and Recreation Department. Hearty meals are served in the dining room, and guest rooms are available on the second floor. Walk into the parlor, furnished with period antiques; notice the sunlight filtering through lace-curtained windows; and imagine a long-skirted matron or young lady sipping a cup of tea while waiting for the next stage to depart.

The dining room is open to the public for breakfast, lunch, and dinner year-round (except New Year's). For information and overnight reservations, write P.O. Box 97, Wolf Creek 97497 or call (503) 866–2474.

Small hamlets and communities like Remote, Camas Valley, Days Creek, Tiller, Lookingglass, Riddle, and Glide contain many descendants of both early miners and pioneers. These folks live in the peaceful, forested valleys and remote areas of the Umpqua River and its tributaries, east and west of Roseburg, the county seat and timber community. There are a few native peoples left, too—a small community of Cow Creek Indians.

One of the region's most pleasant and pastoral bed-and-breakfast experiences is found by travelers near the hamlet of Myrtle Creek, just off Interstate 5 north of Canyonville. Here you can sleep in one of the guest rooms in the main house or in your own private four-room guest cottage at this 400-acre sheep ranch, ◆ **Sonka's Sheep Station Bed and Breakfast.** From the windows of your cozy sitting area, which includes a small kitchen, you'll often see the woolly critters in the lush pasture to the north. Guests enjoy watching the lambing and shearing processes; the kids love petting the small lambs and discovering where wool coats come from.

After breakfast of, say, orange-pecan waffles with wild blackberry syrup, you can, during summer months, enjoy a second cup of coffee on the patio shaded by enormous old maple trees. Often Louis Sonka will show you how Wilkie, the border collie, can round up the sheep in no time at all, in the large pasture just beyond the wide porch that wraps around the fifty-year-old house. For further information and reservations, contact the Sonkas at 901 Northwest Chadwick Lane, Myrtle Creek 97457, or call (503) 863–5168.

Also hidden away on the county roads—look for the bright blue Douglas County road signs with yellow numbers—and in the small valleys near Roseburg are some of the region's first vineyards and wineries. More than thirty years ago the first varietal grapes were planted by Richard Sommer at **Hillcrest Vineyard,** and from these first roots eventually emerged a thriving colony of vintners just west of Roseburg—Davidson Winery, Giradet Wine Cellars, Lookingglass Winery, Callahan Ridge Winery, Hillcrest Vineyard, Umpqua River Vineyards, and Henry Winery.

To reach the wineries, drive through the oak-dotted, rolling hills west of Roseburg. Most of these enterprises are within 20 miles of Roseburg and welcome visitors, although it's best to call ahead to make certain the tasting rooms are open; some of the vineyards are open just by appointment. The visitors' information center in Roseburg will have helpful maps and may be willing to call ahead for you. Those who want to remain on the side roads awhile longer should ask for *A Guide to Historic Barns* and *A Driver's Guide to Historic Places.* Write or stop by the visitors' center at 410 SE Spruce Street (P.O. Box 1262), Roseburg 97756, or call (503) 672–9731.

Wind over to Winston to visit **Wildlife Safari,** a 600-acre, drive-through wild-animal reserve of more than a hundred different species of animals and birds representing Africa, Asia, and other exotic areas of the world. Among the wildlife living here are the Tibetan yak, wildebeest, eland, lion, elephant, ostrich, hippopotamus, rhinoceros, and cheetah.

Since 1980 Wildlife Safari has been operated by the Safari Game Search Foundation, a nonprofit organization dedicated to preserving endangered species, conducting animal-related research, providing educational programs for elementary schools throughout the Northwest, and rehabilitating injured wildlife. A world leader in the research and breeding of cheetahs, the organization has successfully raised nearly one hundred cheetah cubs here in the past fifteen years and is one of the largest providers of cheetahs to zoos throughout the world.

The reserve is open year-round, every day from 9:00 A.M. to dusk. It offers a few spaces with overnight hookups for recreational vehicles. For information about membership in the Safari Game Search Foundation, contact the staff at Wildlife Safari, P.O. Box 1600, Winston 97496 (503–679–6761). The reserve is about 4 miles west of Interstate 5 from the Winston exit.

For exhibits of some of the region's natural history, as well as logging and mining equipment dating from the 1800s, detour from Interstate 5 just south of Roseburg—at the Fairgrounds exit—to visit the **Douglas County Museum of History and Natural History,** located in the large contemporary structure next to the fairgrounds. After poking around the vintage logging and mining equipment in the courtyard, be sure to look inside for the fine exhibit of old photographs. Though the photographs are yellowed with age, the weathered faces in them mirror hope and determination as well as hardship and even heartbreak; the exhibit offers a poignant look into Oregon's pioneer past. The museum is open year-round, Tuesday through Saturday from 10:00 A.M. to 4:00 P.M. and Sunday from noon to 4:00 P.M.; the telephone number is (503) 440–4506. A shady park just next door offers picnic tables and parking for recreational vehicles.

Another side trip from Roseburg weaves east into the southern Cascade Mountains. Highway 138 plays hide-and-seek with the North Umpqua River and with many frothy waterfalls carrying names like Toketee, Lemolo, White Horse, Clearwater, and Steamboat. The falls and nearby parking areas, beginning about 20 miles east of Glide, are well marked. A section of the scenic river, also well marked, is open just to those who love to fly-fish.

If you pass through the community of Glide—it's about 17 miles east of Roseburg—sometime in mid-April and notice lots of cars parked near the Community Building, stop to see whether the annual **Glide Wildflower Show** is in progress. At this show some 300 native plants and flowers from the southern Oregon region are displayed in lovely arrangements by local naturalists and wildflower lovers.

Plan one last detour before entering the lush Willamette Valley region: a stop in the small community of Oakland, nestled in the picturesque hills just north of Roseburg. About twenty-five years ago, when the area's lumber mill closed, Oakland felt an economic decline common to many timber towns throughout the Northwest. The townsfolk's response, though, was decidedly uncommon—they worked to have their circa 1852 community designated the ◆**Oakland Historic District** and placed on the National Register of Historic Places, the first such district in Oregon to be so recognized, in 1967.

Begin with a stroll on Locust Street, poking into a few of its antique shops and boutiques. Then stop at ◆**Tolley's Restaurant and Antiques** for lunch or dinner, during which you'll be surrounded by more antiques, an old-fashioned soda fountain, and a lovely curved staircase of gleaming wood. Romantic candle-lighted tables are on the balcony level. The restaurant and ice-cream parlor are open Tuesday through Sunday from 10:00 A.M. to 10:00 P.M. and on Monday from 10:00 A.M. to 6:00 P.M.; the phone number is (503) 459–1819.

Next browse through memorabilia and old photographs at the **Oakland Museum,** open daily except holidays (503–459–4531), and conclude your visit by walking farther up both sides of Locust Street to see vintage commercial structures, art galleries, antiques shops, and Victorian-style houses. Ask at Tolley's if the Oakland Gaslight Players are doing summertime melodramas in the renovated high school building at the upper end of Locust Street.

SOUTHEASTERN OREGON

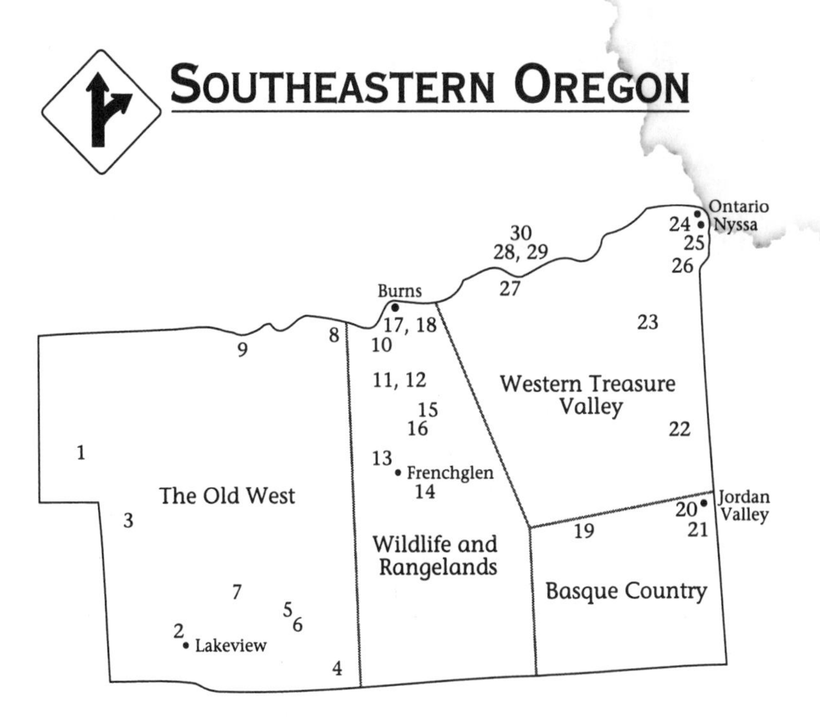

1. Fremont Highway
2. Old Perpetual Geyser
3. Paisley Rodeo
4. Pelican Lake
5. Hart Mountain National Antelope Refuge
6. Hot Springs Campground
7. Abert Rim
8. Sagehen Hill Nature Trail
9. Glass Buttes
10. John Scharff Migratory Water-fowl Festival
11. Malheur National Wildlife Refuge
12. George M. Benson Memorial Museum
13. French Glen Hotel
14. Steens Mountain National Back Country Byway
15. Diamond Craters Natural Area
16. Diamond Hotel
17. Harney County Historical Society Museum
18. Steens Mountain Cafe
19. Rome Columns and Owyhee River
20. Jordan Valley
21. Old Basque Inn Restaurant
22. Leslie Gulch–Succor Creek National Back Country Byway
23. Lake Owyhee and Owyhee Dam
24. Nyssa
25. Wild Horse Roundup
26. Keeney Pass Oregon Trail Site
27. Juntura
28. Beulah Reservoir
29. Chukar Park Campground
30. Castle Rock

SOUTHEASTERN OREGON

THE OLD WEST

Southeastern Oregon is the state's "big sky" country, made up of its three largest and least-populated counties: Harney, Malheur, and Lake. The whole of many states on the East Coast could fit into this wide-open country in the Beaver State's far southeastern corner. In the 28,450-square-mile area containing just Malheur and Lake counties, there are less than ten persons per square mile—now, that's elbow room with room to spare.

The stark, panoramic landscapes here evoke images of western movies; one can easily imagine cowboys riding "Old Red" and "Big Blue," herding cattle through sagebrush-blanketed valleys and across rushing streams and sending scouts up narrow canyons to flat-topped buttes or along alkali lakes far ahead. The horizon stretches wide in all four directions in this massive high-desert country, broken now and then by shaggy pinnacles, ridged rimrock canyons, flat-topped buttes, and massive fault-block mountains.

Hudson's Bay Company explorer-trapper Peter Skene Ogden, along with other fur traders who came in the mid-1820s, had a relative easy time venturing into the region because resident Native Americans had already carved numerous trails, often following deer and antelope trails. The ancient Paiute Indians hunted, traveled the animal trails, gathered seeds, and dug camas bulbs for centuries before Ogden's party arrived in 1826.

Other white people passed through in the 1850s, during the California gold rush. Those early cattle barons then grabbed millions of acres of the southeastern desert country for rangeland in the 1870s and 1880s. The region still contains a number of the old ranches, and raising beef cattle remains one of the primary occupations—along with raising sheep, which were introduced by the immigrant Basques in the 1890s.

In 1843 Captain John C. Frémont, a topographic engineer, was sent to the territory by the U.S. government to explore the region. He is responsible for naming many of the bold features of Lake County encountered during this winter expedition. You can follow his north-south route on Highway 31, the ◆**Fremont Highway,** which is accessed from Lakeview, near the Oregon-California border, or from Highway 97 just south of Bend, near LaPine.

Just 2 miles north of Lakeview off Highway 395, visit **Old Perpetual,** a geyser that spouts about 60 feet above the ground every ninety seconds. The underground water heats to a temperature of some 200 degrees, erupting in a frothy, billowy column. Adjacent to the Sportsman Motel and **Hunter's Hot Springs Resort** is a large lake that steams all year; hundreds of geese and ducks fly in to spend the night, especially during the winter, when other waters are frozen.

If you trek through the area in September, check out the **Lake County Fair,** featuring the largest and oldest amateur rodeo in the Northwest, the **Paisley Rodeo.** You'll notice cowboys and cowgirls riding through the streets of nearby Paisley, a frontier town on the Chewaucan River along the Fremont Highway, and you'll also spot the old watering trough and hitching post downtown. Civilization can't be too far away, though—there's also an airstrip that accommodates small planes here. Further information and current dates for the county fair and rodeo can be obtained from the Lake County Visitors' Information Center, Courthouse Building, Lakeview 97630 (503–947–6040).

If time allows, head east via Highway 140 to see whether the pelican colony is nesting at **Pelican Lake,** about 28 miles east of Lakeview. Turn north at the hamlet of Adel—a restaurant and a gas station are situated here—and proceed on a paved side road for a mile or so. This road continues another 15 miles to the small ranching community of Plush; along the way you might see Canada geese, sandhill cranes, and deer, particularly during the migrations in late fall.

For an alternate and closer route to Plush, head east from Lakeview on Highway 140 for about 15 miles, then turn north and proceed 19 miles to this small ranching community on the edge of Hart Lake that serves as the gateway to **Hart Mountain National Antelope Refuge.** The 275,000-acre federal wildlife refuge was established in 1930, and the mountain was named for the heart-shaped brand of a former cattle ranch located nearby; the word was apparently misspelled. Along its mountain slopes and canyons clothed with groves of graceful aspen, craggy yellow pine, and ground-hugging sagebrush flourishes one of the largest herds of pronghorn antelope in the United States. The larger mule deer, with prominent ears, are seen in the area as well.

Note: The all-weather gravel roads found in this region are often bumpy, steep, and one lane wide; always have a full tank of gas, extra water, and food supplies before heading into the hinterlands. Be prepared to change flat tires as well. Diesel fuel is usually available only in the larger cities, and gas stations along remote stretches close at dusk. The high desert is unforgiving regardless of the season; days can be hot and dry, nights chilly or freezing.

Thus well equipped, you can try out your natural-history–exploring persona and a more relaxed pace while carefully negotiating the narrow all-weather road north of Plush that climbs steeply 27 miles to **Hot Springs Campground,** atop 7,710-foot Hart Mountain. You'll pass the National Refuge headquarters at the top and then continue a short distance to the campground where you can immerse your road-weary body in a natural hot-water spring right next to the sky. The pool is enclosed by a block wall windbreak, roofless to let the stars in—and the night sky is virtually jammed with glittering stars. Pitch your tent, walk the short trail to the summit overlook, and watch for eagles, badgers, and wild bighorn sheep, as well as the antelope and deer that are protected here (they feed in the early morning and at dusk).

The Hart Mountain National Antelope Refuge area is also well-known to rock hounds for its agate nodules, fire opal, crystals, and sun stones. For gem-hunting locations open to the public, check with the ranger at the refuge headquarters; or pick up maps and obtain directions from the visitors' information center in Lakeview (503–947–3315), particularly if you want to go to the sun-stone area. Write to the refuge manager for futher information, P.O. Box 111, Lakeview 97630.

From Plush you can connect with Highway 395 by heading northwest along the hogback for about 31 miles of good all-weather dirt road. In the distance you'll see Coyote Hills and 30-mile-wide **Abert Rim** rising 2,000 feet above the plateau, filling the western horizon along the edge of Abert Lake. Its 800-foot lava cap ends in a sheer precipice.

This scarp is a nearly perfect fault, one of the largest exposed faults in the world. On huge boulders at the base are pictographs drawn by early Indians who lived in the region; arrowheads, rock foundations of primitive huts, and bleached bones have also been discovered in the area.

This southeastern region is dotted with beds of lakes formed thousands of years ago. Some lakes evaporated; others found outlets or were clogged by showers of volcanic ash. Some contain water during the brief rainy season; others are always dry; and still others retain only enough moisture to become meadows. You'll see chalky white alkali around many of the lakes' shores, as the lakes shrink during the summer months.

Head north on paved Highway 395, passing Wagontire and stopping at **Riley,** a distance of about 60 miles. Here mule deer share the browse with shaggy range bulls that look the size of locomotives. Gas up at Riley, or continue east some 25 miles on Highway 20, stopping in the larger community of **Burns** to replenish gas and food supplies.

Just east of Riley you can detour at the rest area and walk the ½ mile ◆**Sagehen Hill Nature Trail** to become acquainted with the native shrubs and plants of the high desert region. At eleven self-guided stations, visitors identify big sagebrush (take a small leaf, rub it between your palms, and whiff the wonderful fragrance); bitterbrush, with its dark green leaves and yellow springtime flowers; western juniper, one of the dominant trees, its blue-green berries loved by many bird species; low sagebrush; and Idaho fescue, an important native bunchgrass that grows on the high desert.

Along the trail you may also see dwarf monkey flower, western yarrow, blue-eyed Mary, owl clover, lupine, and wild parsley. Keep an eye out for red-tailed hawks, golden eagles, turkey vultures, and prairie falcons, as well as sage grouse, mourning doves, mountain bluebirds, and Oregon's state bird, the melodious western meadowlark.

Look toward the west to spot Wagontire Mountain, Squaw Butte, and Glass Buttes. On a clear day you can see Steens Mountain to the south and east; it's composed of hundreds of layers of basalt lava that were thrust more than 1 mile above the plateau about 15 million years ago. Directly south is **Palomino Buttes,** part of a Bureau of Land Management area for wild horses that covers about 96,000 acres. Often bands of from thirty to sixty wild horses are seen along the roads in the area.

Rising some 2,000 feet above the high desert—for a total elevation of 6,385 feet—the great ◆**Glass Buttes** are said to be the largest outcropping of iridescent obsidian in the world. From the glassy lava rock, the native peoples chipped, chiseled, and knapped arrowheads, spear points, scrapers, axes, and other implements. At the Glass Buttes you can see this enormous arrowhead "factory," where tons and tons of chipped obsidian remain, left by generations of Native Americans who passed through the region.

Actually, arrowheads found in the Ohio mounds in the Midwest have been identified as having come from the Glass Buttes of southeastern Oregon. The other primary source of obsidian for early peoples was in the outcroppings of Yellowstone Park in Wyoming. The two kinds of obsidian are easily identified because of their distinctive colorings—the Glass Buttes obsidian is more colorful, its iridescence often a quarter-inch thick. It's called rainbow obsidian.

A close-up view of the Glass Buttes may be accessed from Highway 20 about 17 miles west of Riley on a primitive, unimproved dirt road just west of the buttes. Drive with care for ⅛ mile or so—low-slung automobiles won't do well on unimproved roads—and you'll see the buttes glistening with their iridescent rainbow hues in the afternoon sun. You can learn much more about the native peoples who lived in this region by planning a visit to the Oregon High Desert Museum, just south of Bend (see page 77).

By now even the most confirmed urbanite will have relaxed into the quiet strength of the high desert, and the notion of becoming an amateur geologist or naturalist, even for a brief time, will seem an appealing alternative. These wide-open spaces also had an appeal for an eclectic mix of early settlers—first trappers and miners, then cowboys, cattle barons, and sheepherders, each, of course, displacing the native peoples, many of whom were ultimately sent to reservations.

The cattle barons and sheepherders were, needless to say, on less than friendly terms in those early days, and many bloody skirmishes occurred between the two groups until the federal government intervened. Today nearly 75 percent of the land in southeastern Oregon is managed by the Bureau of Land Management.

WILDLIFE AND RANGELANDS

If your visit to the region coincides with the early spring migration, consider taking in the ◆**John Scharff Migratory Waterfowl Festival** in Burns. Meet bird lovers from all over the Northwest, participate in guided bird-watching walks, see films and slide shows, and hear interesting lectures given by noted waterfowl experts. For dates—the festival usually takes place the first or second weekend of April—write to the Burns-Harney County Visitors' Center, 18 D Street, Burns 97720, or call (503) 573–2636.

Burns, in its earliest years, was the capital of the old cattle empire—the surrounding areas were ruled by cattle barons like Peter French and Henry Miller—but by 1889 Burns amounted to a straggling frontier village of one dusty main street bordered by frame shacks. During the next thirty-five years, the settlers waited for the expanding railroad system to reach their town. A colorful throng gathered to see the first train arrive in September 1924—the cattle ranchers wearing Stetsons, the cowboys sporting jingling spurs on their high-heeled boots, and the Paiute Indians attired in their brightly hued native dress.

Another colorful throng, this one composed of bird species and wildlife, gathers just south of Burns near Harney and Malheur lakes on the ◆**Malheur National Wildlife Refuge.** On your way into the refuge, stop at the National Refuge headquarters for information on current road conditions and which bird species are in residence. The headquarters is located on the south shore of Malheur Lake, 40 miles south of Burns via Highways 78 and 205; the last 6 miles are gravel surfaced. The headquarters and its visitors' center are open weekdays from 8:00 A.M. to 4:30 P.M. Call (503) 493–2612; the mailing address is P.O. Box 245, Princeton 97721. *Note:* Check water and weather conditions on the refuge when planning a visit.

While at the refuge headquarters, stop at the ◆**George M. Benson Memorial Museum,** just next door, where you can see nearly 200 beautifully mounted specimens of migratory birds. The museum is open daily from 6:00 A.M. to 9:00 P.M.

For seminars on local history, geology, and birds and wildlife and for guided trips, folks stay at the **Malheur Field Station,** also located just next to the National Refuge headquarters and the museum. This nonprofit "Desert Wilderness Program" is supported by twenty-two schools and by such prestigious organizations as the Audubon Society, the Nature Conservancy, and the Oregon High Desert Museum in Bend. Outdoor classes for students of all ages, from all over the region, and including Elderhostel programs for seniors sixty and older, are held here year-round.

Travelers can also bunk in one of the trailers or dorm rooms (bring your own sleeping bag) at the Malheur Field Station and can arrange for meals here as well. For information and reservations—the latter are a must, especially during spring and autumn bird migration seasons—write to Director, Malheur Field Station, Box 260-E, Princeton 97721, or call (503) 493–2629.

Use the helpful maps provided by the U.S. Fish and Wildlife Service and the U.S. Department of the Interior as you explore this magnificent wildlife refuge, which received official approval from President Theodore Roosevelt in 1908. The lakes, ponds, marshes, mudflats, and grain crops of the refuge are now managed for the benefit of both resident and migratory wildlife. Prior to this intervention early settlers had engaged in unrestricted hunting of the birds, and plume hunters had nearly wiped out the swans, egrets, herons, and grebes to obtain and sell their elegant feathers to milliners in San Francisco, Chicago, and New York.

Continue south on Highway 205 toward Frenchglen, a journey that will take you through the heart of the refuge, with its 185,000 acres of open water, marshes, irrigated meadows and grainfields, riparian grassy areas, and uplands. You'll first notice antelope bitterbrush, sagebrush, and western juniper, followed by quaking aspen and mountain mahogany at elevations above 4,000 feet.

Although the largest concentration of migratory birds usually occurs in March and April, many varieties can be seen throughout the year here—including the mallards, Canada geese, and greater sandhill cranes that gather noisily to feed in the Blitzen Valley grainfields located just south of National Refuge headquarters, Rattlesnake Butte, and Buena Vista Ponds. Great blue herons, white pelicans, trumpeter swans, long-billed curlews, great egrets, snowy egrets, and many kinds of ducks, geese, and hawks also rest and often nest on the refuge; many of these species can also be seen on the large marshes and ponds near Burns. *Note:* Your car makes an excellent observation and photographic blind; birds will be less frightened if you stay in your car and move slowly. Use binoculars and telephoto lenses; go on your own or join a naturalist-guided tour. In any case you'll soon get used to quantities of bird talk: gabbles, honks, whistles, twitters, low quacking, and the curious rattle-honk of the sandhill cranes. This is archetypal wilderness at its best.

French Glen Hotel

Just south of Malheur and Harney lakes, in the shadow of a commanding, 9,670-foot fault block known as Steens Mountain, tiny **French Glen Hotel** sits like a miniature sentinel reminding visitors of the pioneer past. Built in the late 1870s by the early cattle baron Peter French, the hotel is now owned by the state and managed by the State Parks and Recreation Department. Along with other bird-watchers and photography buffs, you can reserve one of the eight postage stamp–size guest rooms. The evening meal is served family style, accompanied by lively exchanges between guests about fishing exploits, bird-watching areas, wildflower finds, and ghost towns discovered in the area. Next morning the aroma of freshly brewed coffee will lure you downstairs to an enormous breakfast of such delights as giant blueberry pancakes, eggs, sausage, and huge slices of watermelon, cantaloupe, and pineapple. For information—reservations are a must, especially for meals—contact the innkeepers at French Glen Hotel, Frenchglen 97736 (503–493–2825). The hotel is open from March through October.

Naturally, you'll work off this hearty morning meal by poking around the Frenchglen Mercantile; the village has a population of about ten, depending on the time of year, and the number of buildings can be counted on one hand. If you have a hardy vehicle, preferably with four-wheel drive, and want to take in spectacular vistas way off the beaten path, drive the 69-mile **Steens Mountain National Back Country Byway** loop, which begins just 3 miles south of Frenchglen. *Note:* Allow two to three hours for this panoramic drive. There are two campgrounds on the north section of the loop drive.

Check with the Bureau of Land Management visitors' information trailer in Frenchglen for current road conditions—don't attempt this route in rainy or icy weather. On the one-way deeply rutted gravel road, the steep climb through sagebrush to juniper, into groves of quaking aspen, and into alpine wildflower-strewn meadows is deceivingly gradual.

Then you are suddenly next to the sky, at nearly 10,000 feet above the desert floor, and are pulling off at **East Rim Viewpoint** to gaze at ancient glaciated valleys and down at the Alvord Desert, more than a mile below. Keep an eye out for kestrels, golden eagles, bald eagles, prairie falcons, bighorn sheep, and deer during summer months—and black rosy finches at the summit.

If the Steens Mountain loop drive seems a bit strenuous for your automobile, consider the easier, 26-mile **Diamond Loop.** This latter trek is reached from an 18-mile side road, a section of the **Blitzen Valley Auto Tour Route,** as you head east from the Malheur National Refuge headquarters—where you can pick up a brochure for this self-guided auto tour.

On this western section of Diamond Loop, stop at **Diamond Craters Natural Area** for a self-guided hike through lava cones, ropy lava flows, cinder cones, spatter cones, and other unusual volcanic remnants scattered over several square miles. For current regional maps, auto guides, and hiking information, contact the Burns District Bureau of Land Management office, 12533 Highway 20 West, Hines 97738, or call (503) 573–5241.

At the northeast corner of Diamond Loop, you can see one of the state's oldest, most unusual structures: a round barn built a hundred or so years ago by cattle baron Peter French. It was used for breaking horses during winter months. Besides several willow and stockade fences, the only other structure remaining of

French's cattle empire is the Long Barn, which you can walk through at the historic P Ranch location near Frenchglen.

From 1872, when he arrived with a herd of cattle and six Mexican vaqueros, until 1897, Peter French expanded his holdings and cattle operation to the point where he controlled nearly 200,000 acres, ran some 45,000 head of cattle and more than 3,000 horses, and built a dozen ranches encircling his domain on the west side of Steens Mountain. (Rulers of the enormous areas to the north and east were cattle barons John Devine and Henry Miller.) Peter French and his partner were fatally shot by disgruntled neighboring ranchers on the day after Christmas in 1897.

For a comfortable overnight stay about as far into the hinterlands as you can drive, located at the south end of the Diamond Loop Drive, the **Diamond Hotel** offers five small bedrooms on the second floor with baths down the hall, like the "olden days." The hostelry does extra duty as general store, deli, and post office for Diamond's six or so enthusiastic residents. These include Judy and Jerry Santillie, the couple who purchased the building in 1986 and who spent five years renovating it. Hearty family-style dinners are served to hotel guests at 6:30 P.M. or, a bit later, at 7:30 P.M. for a lighter offering of, say, salad and hearty soups. The hotel is open March through October. For information and reservations contact the Santillies at P.O. Box 10, Diamond 97722, or call them at (503) 493–1898. If the hotel is filled, check with the folks at **McCoy Creek Inn** (503–493–2131), the only other overnight accommodation in the immediate area except for Frenchglen and the dormitory lodging at Malheur Field Station. Burns, however, offers several motels such as Best Western Ponderosa (503–573–2047). *Note:* Remember that distances in this remote section of the Beaver State are deceiving and that food and gasoline services are also remote and many hours apart. Always have current state maps, keep track of distances and time of day, refill your gas tank before heading into the sagebrush and alkali desert country, and arrange ahead for overnight accommodations (unless you are camping).

The **Harney County Historical Society Museum** in Burns contains many informational displays and vintage photographs that allow a peek into this fascinating Old West section of Oregon. The museum, located at 18 West D Street in Burns

(503–573–2636) is open from June through September, Tuesday through Saturday from 9:00 A.M. to 5:00 P.M.

If your travel schedule or the weather conditions prevent a trip from Burns into the Malheur National Wildlife Refuge and Peter French's historic Blitzen Valley, try the shorter **Lower Silvies River Valley Drive,** via Highway 78, just southeast of Burns in the scenic Harney Valley. Here you can see ducks, geese, and sandhill cranes in March and April and can observe avocets, ibis, terns, curlews, and egrets through July.

Before heading out of Burns, however, stop at **Steens Mountain Cafe.** Tony Diaz, owner and chef, uses old-fashioned Basque recipes and serves the kind of family-style meals you would have been served at a Basque boardinghouse years ago. His father, seventy-two-year-old Avel Diaz, now retired, was one of the colony of Basque sheepherders who settled in this remote corner of the state. The eight-course meal includes soup, salad, wine, meat, vegetables, rice, and freshly baked Basque breads. "Folks eat till their tummies are happy," says Tony. For dessert be sure to order flan, the traditional Spanish custard. The rustic restaurant is located at 195 N. Alder Street, Burns 97720, and the hours are from 11:00 A.M. to 2:00 P.M. and from 5:00 to 9:00 P.M., Tuesday through Saturday. The telephone number is (503) 573–7226.

For information about hiking on the high desert, contact the Desert Trail Association, P.O. Box 589, Burns 97720.

From Burns you can head east on Highway 20 toward Ontario and the Oregon-Idaho border; west on Highway 20 toward Bend and central Oregon's high desert country; southwest via Highway 78 toward Jordan Valley; or continue south via Highways 78 and 95 to the Oregon-Nevada border.

BASQUE COUNTRY

At Burns Junction, about 92 miles southeast of Burns, turn east on Highway 95. After roughly 15 miles turn north on a gravel-surfaced road just beyond the hamlet of Rome and opposite the Owyhee Canyon Road sign. The intriguing **Rome Columns** can be seen from a viewpoint about 3½ miles down the dusty road. The columns are huge formations of sandstone and fossil-bearing clay from Oregon's prehistoric past that jut some 1,000 feet into the intense blue sky. Surrounded by yellow-blooming sagebrush, the creamy-colored battlements, stained with rich browns, overlook the peaceful ranch and farm valley of the nearby **Owyhee River.**

Actually, eons ago this high desert area was a lush tropical paradise, as evidenced by many species of shell and animal fossils found throughout the layers of ancient riverbeds and lake beds. Those emigrant pioneers who detoured south through this region in the early 1840s carved their names in the soft sandstone; later, the area also served as a stage stop.

Just north of the bridge, across the Owyhee River, you could turn right to the Bureau of Land Management guard station, which has a small grassy area, picnic tables, potable water, and a rest room. There is also a public boat ramp here.

Just 33 miles east of Rome, the community of **Jordan Valley** sits at an elevation of 4,389 feet, virtually on the Oregon-Idaho border. This small town became the unlikely home of a band of Basque emigrants who in the 1890s left their homelands in the French and Spanish Pyrenees. The Basques, being sheepherders, also brought lambs and ewes to the Jordan Valley. By the turn of the century—and after countless bloody skirmishes—sheepherding replaced cattle ranching in this far southeastern corner of the state.

Originally an important way station on a supply line between the mining camps of California and Idaho, Jordan Valley thus became a major sheep-trading center and the home of the Basque settlers and their families. Near the old Jordan Valley Hotel in the center of town, you can see remnants of a hand-hewn stone court where early Basque townspeople played pelota, an energetic game similar to handball.

Stop at the **Old Basque Inn Restaurant** for tasty local food; the eatery is located in town on North Highway 95 (503–586–2298) and is open daily from 6:00 to 10:00 P.M. For an overnight stay, try the Sahara Motel (503–586–2500) or the Basque Station Motel (503–586–9244). Other than camping, these two motels are the only overnight options in the Jordan Valley area.

For current information about the region, about the annual Jordan Valley Big Loops Rodeo, held each May, and about other colorful Basque festivals held during summer and fall, contact the Nyssa Visitors' Information Center, 212 Main Street (P.O. Box 2515), Nyssa 97913 (503–372–3091).

WESTERN TREASURE VALLEY

From Jordan Valley head north on Highway 95 about 18 miles, turning onto an all-weather gravel road that angles northwest toward ◆ **Leslie Gulch–Succor Creek National Back Country Byway.** The rugged road—accessible to all but low-slung automobiles, which won't do so well—drops into a canyon where sandstone cliffs seem to loom higher, as well as to hover closer together. Their deep pinks, flamboyant purples, vibrant oranges, and flaming reds splash across the brilliant blue sky, the stark landscape littered here and there with pungent sage and bitterbrush. This scenery is guaranteed to buckle the knees of the toughest cowpoke or the most cynical urban dweller.

Miles of dirt roads and trails are available to hikers, backpackers, and off-road vehicles in the Leslie Gulch area, managed by the Bureau of Land Management. You can see wild horses and bighorn sheep roaming through the canyons, as well as chukars (small partridges) dashing across dusty roadbeds and up steep talus slopes. Look for thunder eggs—oblong rocks, rough on the outside but usually containing beautiful crystal formations on the inside—at nearby **Succor Creek Canyon,** and look for agates along the banks of the Owyhee River. The best time to visit is April through June, although snow is possible in early May. Summers are hot and dry, with temperatures of 90 degrees and above, whereas by late September the nights are frosty. *Note:* There are rest rooms and drinking water at the Succor Creek Recreation Area Campground; rest rooms and camping but no water at Leslie Gulch. Check for ticks after hiking—they can carry Lyme disease. For current information check with the Vale District Office of the Bureau of Land Management, 100 Oregon Street, Vale 97018 (503–473–3144).

Primitive campgrounds are available both in Leslie Gulch and, 17 miles north of Leslie Gulch, at Succor Creek State Recreation Area, but you'll need to haul in your own drinking water. A better alternative is the campground just south of Owyhee Dam at Lake Owyhee State Park, on the shores of ◆ **Lake Owyhee**—about 23 miles from Adrian, off Highway 201 (Adrian is about 20 miles north of Succor Creek State Recreation Area). Another alternative is to call ahead to arrange motel-with-kitchen accommodations at **Lake Owyhee Resort** (503) 339–2444. Services here include a small store with fishing tackle, some food, maps of reservoir and fishing areas, pontoon boat rentals, and a few cabins, as well as motel rooms.

If you plan a trip into this remote area, be sure to have a full tank of gas, plenty of food and beverages, sturdy shoes, and camping gear. There are a few electrical hookups at Lake Owyhee State Park, as well as a public boat ramp and a dock. The toll-free (within Oregon but outside the Portland metropolitan area) Campsite Information center phone number is 800–452–5687; to call the center from Portland or from outside the state, call (503) 238–7488. The information center is open from the first Monday in March to Labor Day, 8:00 A.M. to 4:30 P.M.

Be sure to stop and see the imposing **Owyhee Dam,** located north of the campground. Begun in 1926 and completed in 1932, the dam rises 405 feet from bedrock, is 255 feet thick at its base in the sandstone and basalt canyon, and is 30 feet thick at the top. The structure represents one of the largest and most important irrigation developments in the state, for the Owyhee River waters stored in the large lake behind the dam are used not only for year-round recreation but also to irrigate an extensive area of high desert that would otherwise remain an arid wasteland.

Near the communities of Nyssa, Vale, and Ontario—located on the Oregon-Idaho border about 45 miles north of Owyhee Dam and Lake Owyhee—you can see evidence of the Owyhee River waters bringing life to lush fields of sugar beets, potatoes, onions, and alfalfa. Notice the tall green poplars and the shaggy locusts around homesteads, then rows of fruit trees gradually giving way to wheat and grazing lands.

In **Nyssa,** a thriving community for the dairy and poultry industries, a large beet-sugar refining plant also produces and ships many tons of sugar each day. Between the three communities of Nyssa, Vale, and Ontario, you can see broad fields of blooming zinnias, bachelor buttons, and other flowers grown for the garden seed market; vegetables are grown here, too. Midsummer is a good time to see the fields of flowers in gorgeous bloom—and you might also smell the pungent, dark-green peppermint plants that cover large fields as well.

In the sagebrush-covered rimrock hills above these beautiful fields, Basque sheepherders sing and echo their distinctive native melodies while they and their sheepdogs tend large flocks. Many

Mexican-American families also live in the area, as do a large number of Japanese-Americans, who resettled here following the forced internments in the area during World War II. For information and current dates for the colorful annual ethnic festivals held in the area, contact the Ontario Visitors' Information Center, 173 SW First Street, Ontario 97914 (503–889–8012); the Nyssa Visitors' Information Center, 212 Main Street (P.O. Box 2515), Nyssa 97913 (503–372–3091); and the Vale Visitors' Information Center, 275 North Main Street (P.O.Box 661), Vale 97918 (503–473–3800).

You might also be interested in the annual ◆**Wild Horse Roundup** coordinated by the Bureau of Land Management for the national Adopt-a-Horse program. For the particulars and regulations, inquire at the bureau's Vale district office, P.O. Box 700, Vale 97018 (503–473–3144).

From nearby Nyssa travel west and north on Enterprise Avenue, which is actually a section of the Oregon Trail. Stop at the ◆**Keeney Pass Oregon Trail Site** and look up and down the draw at the deep wagon ruts cut into the soft clay. Here you can also read about some of the hardships experienced. From Amelia Knight's diary entry dated August 5–8, 1853, for example, you'll read this: "Just reached Malheur River and campt, the roads have been very dusty, no water, nothing but dust and dead cattle all day."

For the pioneers the hot mineral springs near Vale were a welcome stop for bathing and washing clothes. At the **Malheur Crossing** marker, located between the bridges on the east edge of Vale, notice the deep ruts left by the heavy wagons pulling up the grade after crossing the river.

The pioneers actually entered what is now Oregon at old Fort Boise—in Idaho, just a few miles east of Nyssa—a fur-trading post established in 1834 by the British Hudson's Bay Company. Here the wagons forded the Snake River, the settlers often having to remove the wheels before the wagons could float across. From Malheur Crossing, where the pioneers enjoyed a welcome soak in the hot springs, the wagon trains continued northwest, met the Snake River again at Farewell Bend, and then made their way through the Snake River Valley and west toward The Dalles and the most difficult river passage from there downriver to Fort Vancouver—the mighty Columbia River.

An alternate route, the old **Central Oregon Emigrant Trail,** is followed rather closely by Highway 20 east from Vale, just north of Keeney Pass. In 1845 an unfortunate wagon train of some 200 pioneers, led by Stephen Meek, first attempted this route. About seventy members of the group died from hardship and exposure when the wagon train wandered for weeks on the high desert, bewildered by the maze of similar ridges, canyons, and washes. Meek was attempting to find a shortcut to the Willamette Valley. The survivors finally reached the Deschutes River, near Bend, and followed it to The Dalles.

Take Highway 20 toward Burns for a nostalgic look at more of the wagon ruts, as well as a view of the vast sagebrush desert those first pioneers struggled to cross. Later, between 1864 and 1868, the **Cascade Mountain Military Road** was laid out following the Emigrant Trail. This new road connected with the old **Willamette Valley Road,** which brought travelers across the central Cascade Mountains to Albany, in the lush Willamette Valley.

In those days wagon trains, some a half-mile long, carried wool and livestock from the eastern Oregon range country to the Willamette Valley, returning with fruit, vegetables, and other food supplies. Stagecoaches, conveying both mail and passengers, added their own dramatic chapter to the history of the Cascade Mountain Military Road. Every settlement on the route drew all or part of its livelihood from this transportation link. Historians, by the way, note that the first automobile to cross the United States was driven over this route, in June 1905.

As you now speed along modern Highway 20 between Vale and Burns, a drive of about two hours, note that this same trip took two full days and one night for the stagecoaches to complete. The tedious trip was continuous, with a change of horses taking place every 15 miles.

About midway between Vale and Burns, you'll pass through ◆**Juntura,** a poplar-shaded village nestled in a small valley where the North Fork of the Malheur River joins the South Fork. Stop to see the lambing sheds near the railroad tracks. Long a major shipping point for both sheep and cattle, the entire valley and surrounding range country were once dominated by the legendary Henry Miller, one of the powerful cattle barons of the late 1800s.

You can see a shearing and dipping plant by turning south from Juntura on an all-weather gravel road and then proceeding for about 4 miles, toward the tiny community of Riverside. For camping or a late-afternoon picnic, head north from Juntura to ◆ **Beulah Reservoir.** The Bureau of Land Management's ◆ **Chukar Park Campground,** situated on the North Fork of the Malheur River, has nineteen sites; the county has a primitive campground on the lake as well. *Note:* Drinking water needs to be packed in here.

About 4 miles north of the campground, find a good area for day hikes at ◆ **Castle Rock,** an extinct volcano cone that rises to an elevation of 6,837 feet. For maps and further information about Chukar Park Campground, day hiking, and fall hunting in the area, contact the bureau's Vale District Office, P.O. Box 700, Vale 97018 (503–473–3144).

Central and Northeastern Oregon

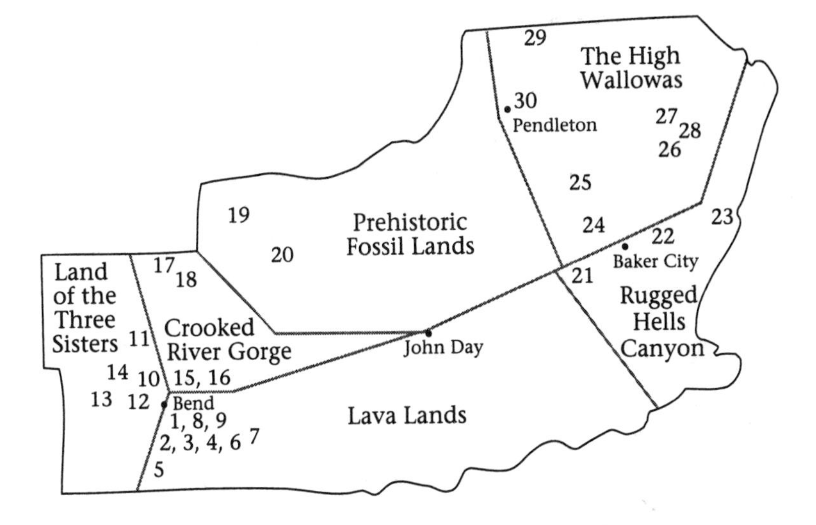

1. Pilot Butte
2. Oregon High Desert Museum
3. Lava Butte
4. Lava Cast Forest
5. Newberry Crater Auto Tour
6. Lava River Cave
7. Pine Mountain Observatory
8. Pine Tavern Restaurant
9. Deschutes Historical Center
10. Tumalo Feed Company
11. Black Butte Ranch
12. Cascade Lakes Scenic Drive
13. Three Sisters Wilderness
14. Metolius-Windigo Trail
15. Redmond Smokejumper Base
16. Juniper Golf Club
17. Kah-Nee-Tah Resort
18. Museum at Warm Springs
19. Historic Shaniko Hotel
20. John Day Fossil Beds National Monument
21. Sumpter Valley Narrow Gauge Railroad
22. National Historic Oregon Trail Interpretive Center
23. Hells Canyon National Recreation Area
24. Haines Steak House
25. Stang Manor Inn
26. Wallowa Lake Tramway
27. Bed, Bread & Trail Inn
28. Valley Bronze Foundry
29. Frazier Farmstead Museum and Gardens
30. Pendleton Underground

Central and Northeastern Oregon

Lava Lands

Carpeted with pungent sagebrush, juniper, and ponderosa pine, Oregon's central high desert country offers generous amounts of sunshine and miles of wide-open spaces at elevations of 3,000 feet and higher. Where ancient Indian fires once blazed on the shores of volcanic lakes and long-ago hunters left tracks and trails through pine and juniper forests, both Oregonians and out-of-staters now come to fish, hunt, camp, and hike. Climbing high rocks and mountains, spelunking in lava tube caves, and going alpine as well as cross-country skiing offer more adventurous outdoor pursuits.

The first white people to venture into central Oregon were hunters who trapped beaver for their lush pelts. Captain John C. Frémont, a topographic engineer, was sent from the East Coast to map the region in the 1840s, although both Peter Skene Ogden and Nathaniel Wyeth traveled through the area before Frémont's trek.

Lured by succulent meadows and grasses, the first immigrants to settle in the region raised cattle and sheep, and many ranches still operate in the area. Although Indian chief Paulina and his Paiute tribe fought against white settlement, peace eventually won out. Named for the old chief, the Paulina Mountains, rising south of Bend, offer a reminder of an important chapter in the area's colorful history.

To get your bearings when arriving in Bend—the largest city and hub of the central region—start from the downtown area and drive to the top of nearby ◆ **Pilot Butte,** at an elevation of 3,400 feet. Here you'll have a panoramic view of not only this sprawling mountain resort community but no fewer than a dozen gorgeous snow-capped volcanic peaks to the west, in the Cascade Range.

These peaks rise along the far horizon like vanilla ice-cream cones. Notice first the largest "double scoopers"—Mt. Jefferson, Mt. Washington, Broken Top, Three Sisters, Mt. Bachelor, and Ollalie Butte. Dusty and tired members of the pioneer wagon trains, as they lumbered across the harsh, unforgiving high desert, used to sight on Pilot Butte so as to maintain their bearings after having crossed the Snake River near the present communities of Ontario, Nyssa, and Vale in the eastern section of the state. Today the road to the top of Pilot Butte is paved, and the viewpoint area is wheelchair-accessible.

For one of the best introductions to the natural history of this vast, unique region, visit the **Oregon High Desert Museum,** just 5 miles south of Bend via Highway 97 toward Lava Butte. On the 150-acre site you can investigate a rimrock canyon, a marsh area, meadows, a flowing stream, a prehistoric cave, and other natural habitats for plants, birds, and wildlife native to the high desert. Self-guided interpretive paths shoelace in and around each life zone. You'll be able to tell a chipmunk from a ground squirrel—both have stripes along their backs, but the chipmunks have stripes on their cheeks, too—before arriving at the main entrance of the orientation center. "It's the relationship between people, the animals, and the desert habitat that we hope visitors come to understand and appreciate," explains Donald Kerr, the museum's director.

Beginning the project with a seed grant of $5,000 in 1977, Kerr and his staff—with the help of educators, private citizens, and businesspersons throughout the Northwest—raised several million dollars for the development of this extraordinary living museum. A dedicated group of volunteers from Bend and many surrounding communities donate countless hours to help maintain the grounds and develop year-round educational programs for children and adults.

Watch mischievous river otters frolic in their indoor-outdoor pool; pet friendly porcupines like "Cuddles" and "Thistlebritches"; and peer into the trunk of a ponderosa pine and hear museum staff and volunteers tell about gopher snakes, birds of prey, or desert weather patterns. The kids will also enjoy the "touching table" covered with the pelts of high-desert animals—beaver, mole, weasel, and coyote. You can even touch a gopher snake if you're so inclined. A Paiute Indian wickiup made of native willow and yellow flowering bitterbrush displays ancient carving and hunting tools around its outdoor campfire.

The latest group of exhibits at the museum complex can be seen in the new Earle A. Chiles Center, offering a nostalgic dawn-to-dusk walk through eight historic scenes portraying the sights, sounds, and smells of the settling of the West—from early Native Americans to the wagon trains, a settler's cabin, and cowboy days.

For a schedule of workshops and special events offered year-round, contact the Oregon High Desert Museum, 59800 S. Highway 97, Bend 97702 (503–382–4754). The museum is open daily, except on major holidays, from 9:00 A.M. to 5:00 P.M.

For another panoramic view of the region, continue south from Bend along Highway 97 for about 10 miles to **Lava Butte,** stopping first at the **Lava Lands Visitors' Center** at its base for an intriguing look at the region's volcanic past. Colorful, animated displays simulate natural phenomena such as a volcanic eruption and an earthquake. You can also walk the **Trail of the Molten Land** or the **Trail of the Whispering Pines,** both short self-guided treks near the visitors' center. Managed by the Deschutes National Forest, the well-stocked center is open May through October from 9:00 A.M. to 4:00 P.M. daily; the telephone number is (503) 593–2421.

The road leading up to 500-foot Lava Butte, the extinct reddish-brown volcanic cone looming above the visitors' center, is steep but well paved with red cinder rock, and there's a large parking area at the top. With camera or binoculars in hand, walk the easy self-guided trail around the top of the butte for spectacular views of ancient lava fields to the north and south and of those ever-present ice-cream-cone mountain peaks.

You're now gazing at a vast area in which folks have lived for more than 9,000 years. The earliest visitors probably came from the Great Basin area of Idaho and Utah to hunt and gather food. About 7,000 years ago the eruptions of Mt. Mazama—now Crater Lake, to the south—and nearby Mt. Newberry produced about 200 times the amount of ash, pumice, and debris created by the eruption of Mount St. Helens in Washington State in 1980. As you continue walking around the rim of Lava Butte, you can also see the Paulina Mountains, Newberry Crater, and the latter's two alpine lakes, Paulina and East lakes, directly to the south and east.

If time allows, head south on Highway 97 and take the 10-mile side trip into **Lava Cast Forest,** winding east through ponderosa pine, bitterbrush, and manzanita on a red cinder gravel road into the high-desert hinterlands. Access from Highway 97, turning east on Forest Service Road 9420, near the Sun River turnoff. Pick up an illustrated guide at the beginning of the paved trail and enjoy twelve descriptive stops along the easy 1-mile trek. As you walk the path, notice the characteristic cinnamon-colored bark of the tall ponderosa pine; then, as you reach the sunny, open lava plain, notice the smaller version of the pine, nature's own bonsai, or dwarf, trees.

Though short and stunted—struggling to grow in the "a-a" (AH-ah) lava, with its rough, jagged, and clinkerlike surfaces—the trees may actually be very old, their root systems enlarged to help fight the extreme environment. You'll also see dead trees bleached white by the desert weather, stark skeletons hunched in the black lava. During spring, flowering wild currant and bitterbrush ornament the volcanic landscape with pale pinks and yellows. Look, too, for red Indian paintbrush and rock pentstemons blooming in crevices and crannies.

Take a moment to imagine how those wagon trains and early pioneers could possibly have crossed the inhospitable lava fields of the high desert during the mid-1840s and the 1850s. The trappers, hunters, and Indians who preceded them were probably better off on foot or horseback, in comparison with having to guide the bulky, oxen- or horse-pulled covered wagons. The rough "a-a" lava surely holds many heart-wrenching memories, particularly of mothers with small children, of those early crossings.

Peer into vertical and horizontal tree casts that about 6,000 years ago were enormous pines engulfed with slow-moving molten lava from **Mt. Newberry.** At station 9 along the trail you can actually see the source of the lava flow, toward what remains of the mountain, to the southeast. The rounded cylindrical casts are the only remnants of the lush forest that once clothed Mt. Newberry's slopes. Station 11 offers another grand view of the other snowcapped peaks in the Cascade Mountain Range, to the west.

Although there is no potable water at Lava Cast Forest, there are a couple of picnic tables, as well as an outdoor rest room, in the shade of tall ponderosa pine. You'll also find a few benches along the trail, affording sunny spots for a picnic lunch in the company of those intriguing tree casts, oddly shaped pine bonsais, and other specimens of plant life. Be sure to pack in drinking water or canned beverages, especially on warm summer days, when temperatures can climb to the eighties or nineties.

Further information about this geologic phenomenon can be obtained from the Deschutes National Forest headquarters in Bend, at 1645 Highway 20 East, or call (503) 388–2715. The office is open year-round, Monday through Friday, from 7:45 A.M. to 4:30 P.M.

For a closer look at the remains of Mt. Newberry, drive to the start of **Newberry Crater Auto Tour,** just 8 miles south of the Sun River turnoff, and wind about 13 miles up to a pair of high mountain lakes bulging with trout—Paulina and East lakes. When 9,000-foot Mt. Newberry collapsed in a fiery roar, a large caldera, 4 to 5 miles across, was formed; it was blocked by further eruptions, creating two lakes rather than the single lake exemplified by, say, Crater Lake to the south.

East Lake is known for producing some of the largest trout ever caught in the United States; both enormous German brown and eastern brook trout weighing in at more than twenty-five pounds have been reeled in here by dedicated anglers. Both lakes have campgrounds and boat docks, and both offer fishing boats and motors for rent. At **Paulina Lake** there is also a rustic lodge, as well as rowboats and fishing equipment for rent. Because legal seasons, bag limits, and types of tackle are highly variable, anglers who want to get licenses to fish the many lakes and rivers in central Oregon are advised to obtain current copies of the official regulations from the Oregon Department of Fish and Wildlife, P.O. Box 59, Portland 97207 (503–229–5403).

Although the first white person to see the two lakes was explorer Peter Skene Ogden, in 1826, he didn't find those wily trout. Fish were introduced into both lakes years later by the State Fish and Game Department; the fish hatchery is near Sisters and Black Butte. The mountain was named for John Strong Newberry, a physician and noted geologist who accompanied the Williamson expedition in 1855 to explore possible railroad routes through the central section of the state.

As you bask in the warm sun on the boat dock at Paulina Lake at a level of 6,331 feet, inside Newberry's crater, notice the large peak looming some 2,000 feet higher into the deep blue sky—that's Paulina Peak, also named for the Paiute Indian chief Paulina. If you're itching to bring your horse to the high desert, you'll find riding trails here, too, and you can bunk at the nearby **Chief Paulina Horse Camp.** For a bit more comfortable lodging, you can stay at **Paulina Lake Resort** in one of a dozen rustic knotty-pine housekeeping cabins. The lodge restaurant serves lunches and dinners and a Saturday night barbecue. For information and reservations call (503) 536–2240; the address is P.O. Box 7, LaPine 97739. The resort is open summers for fishing and December through March for snowmobiling and cross-country skiing.

Serious anglers most often stay at **East Lake Fishing Resort,** P.O. Box 95, LaPine 97739 (503–536–2230), where there are eleven cabins with kitchens. A small restaurant serves breakfast and lunch, and the resort is open mid-May through mid-October. There is also a Forest Service campground at East Lake, with campsites available on a first-come, first-served basis. *Note:* This is a busy place during July and August.

Before retracing your route back to Highway 97, detour on the marked Forest Service side road located between the two lakes to see the large lava flow of glassy black obsidian used by native peoples to fashion arrowheads and other implements; lovely **Paulina Creek Falls** is close by as well. During winter the main paved road into the lakes is plowed for the first 10 miles to the Sno-Park parking area, allowing for backcountry snowmobiling and cross-country skiing; Sno-Park permits can be purchased in Bend or LaPine. This entire 56,000-acre geologic area has been designated the **Newberry National Volcanic Monument.**

While exploring Oregon's high desert country, you must go spelunking in at least one lava cave. The most accessible is ◆ **Lava River Cave,** located in **Lava River Caves State Park,** just off Highway 97 north of Sun River and Lava Cast Forest. With lantern in hand—lanterns are available for a nominal fee at the park entrance station—and sturdy shoes on your feet, proceed toward the cave's yawning entrance. The trail drops over volcanic rocks, bridged by stairs, leading to the floor of the first large, cool chamber. There you might see stalactites and stalagmites of ice, which often don't melt completely until late June or early July.

Negotiate another stairway up to the main tunnel and walk the winding passageway, your lantern reflecting ghostly shadows all along the way. The enormous cave is in places nearly 60 feet high and 50 feet wide, larger than the tunnels beneath New York's Hudson River. Conversations echo from the cave's farthest recesses, returning as eerie voices from the darkness.

Geologists explain that the great cavernous tunnel, which runs for about 5,000 feet through solid lava, was once the course of a molten lava river. Along the walls are remnants of the lava current—slaggy crusts in some places, rounded and overhanging cornicelike shelves in other places, marking the various levels of old volcanic streams. Notice the walls coated with glaze of varying smoothness and, from the ceiling, "lavacicles," volcanic stalactites formed by dripping lava.

Lava River Cave, located about 12 miles south of Bend, is open from May through September, from 9:00 A.M. to 4:00 P.M. daily. Picnic facilities are available in the park, but no drinking water is provided. If you want to go spelunking on your own, access Forest Service Road 18 (also called China Hat Road) just a mile or so south of Bend, driving about 14 miles east to see **Arnold Ice Cave, Skeleton Cave,** and **Wind Cave.** The early settlers of Bend quarried huge chunks of ice from Arnold Ice Cave, hauling it to town on horse-drawn wagons; for about 10 years this ice was the primary method of refrigeration for Bend residents. Since that time, thick layers of ice have reformed and crept upward, fingerlike, blocking the lower stairway. You can peer into the icy darkness safely from the upper stairway near the cave's wide entrance.

Nearby Skeleton Cave is a large, spacious, dry cave a mile or so long and extending some 600 feet into the ground. It's an easy walk for people of most ages, provided that the visitor wears sturdy shoes and uses a lantern or a strong flashlight. The cave's floor is mostly fine lava sand, strewn with lava rocks of various sizes and shapes. *Note:* There is no water here, and you need to bring your own lanterns or flashlight.

Novice spelunkers should note the following safety tips: Explore caves in a group, never alone; bring an ample supply of light sources—a lantern and/or a powerful flashlight for each member of the party; also take candles and matches; dress warmly—lava caves are rarely warmer than 45 degrees, even on hot summer days. Further information can be obtained from the Deschutes National Forest headquarters in Bend.

For another spectacle, this one next to the nighttime sky at the 6,300-foot level, head east from Bend via Highway 20 about 35 miles to **Pine Mountain Observatory,** where you can snoop at the moon, the planets, star clusters, nebulas, and galaxies through a 15-inch research telescope managed by students and instructors from the University of Oregon. In addition to the 15-inch telescope are two other Cassegrain telescopes, with mirrors of 24 and 32 inches, respectively, that are used by the staff to collect research on the planets and stars.

Just beyond the Millican gas station, turn south on the all-weather gravel road, take the right fork near the base of the mountain, and wind 9 miles up to the parking area next to the sky. Though the Pine Mountain Observatory is usually open Friday and Saturday, with viewing at dusk, visitors are asked always to call ahead—(503) 382–8331, after 3:00 P.M.—to make arrangements before driving out to the observatory. Stargazers are advised to wear warm clothing, bring flashlights, and dim their car's headlights as they approach the parking area.

Before leaving the Bend region, consider having lunch or dinner at one of Bend's oldest eateries, the ◆**Pine Tavern Restaurant,** overlooking **Mirror Pond** on the Deschutes River near Drake Park. Several 125-foot ponderosa pines grow right in the middle of the pondside dining room. A mere 250 years old, the cinnamon-barked trees blend nicely with the room's rustic decor and have been growing right through the roof for about fifty years. Especially tasty are the warm sourdough scones with delicious honey butter; they're similar to the Indian fry bread served on the Warm Springs Indian Reservation. Located downtown, the restaurant is open for lunch Monday through Saturday from 11:30 A.M. to 2:30 P.M., for dinner every day from 5:30 to 10:00 P.M. For dinner reservations, call (503) 382–5581.

While in the downtown area, stop by the ◆**Deschutes Historical Center,** situated in the 1914 Reid School building that was placed on the National Register of Historic Places in 1979. Among the fine displays are old farm tools; well-used pioneer crockery; native arrowheads; thunder eggs, Oregon's state rock; and a 530-page chronicle of the region's early history that was compiled by sifting through old family records and census data. The center is open Wednesday through Saturday from 1:00 to 4:00 P.M.; its phone number is (503) 389–1813.

Stop at Drake Park and Mirror Pond to enjoy a front-row seat for watching the goings-on of waterfowl families of all kinds, sizes, and shapes, including graceful swans, colorful mallards, and curious Canada geese. "Act One begins around sunrise," explains one longtime resident, "when duck parents herd their feathered ducklings around the rim of the pond in search of morning tidbits."

You can observe all this bustling activity while eating a picnic lunch at one of the wooden tables scattered here and there in the park. If you have a canoe, save time for a leisurely paddle on the lovely pond. You could also call the staff at Bend Metro Parks and Recreation for information about canoeing classes, held during spring, summer, and fall. The address is 200 Pacific Park Lane, Bend 97701; or you can call them at (503) 389–7275.

For helpful brochures and information about overnight lodging in the Bend area, contact the Central Oregon Reservation Center, Box 230, Bend 97709 (503–389–8799).

LAND OF THE THREE SISTERS

Heading west from Bend on Highway 20, you'll find that the Three Sisters—**South Sister, Middle Sister,** and **North Sister**—form a stunning backdrop against the deep blue sky of central Oregon as you make your way to Sisters, Black Butte, and the headwaters of the Metolius River. The snowy peaks of these three mountains form an elegant trio that seems to be enjoying a sisterly gossip session—or perhaps afternoon tea with a favorite aunt.

If you haven't yet had supper, stop by the ♦**Tumalo Feed Company,** a steak house and old-fashioned saloon, to dine at vintage round oak tables that probably held many a family meal at the turn of the century. Peer into the Bonanza Room for a glimpse of the polished mahogany bar, brought in from a real Nevada ghost town; stained-glass windows, transported from a nineteenth-century territorial mansion; and elegant red plush Victorian parlor chairs. The restaurant is definitely for families, however, and serves dinner family style. Your meal begins with a basket of warm garlic bread, a skillet of fried potatoes, and a bowl of hearty ranch beans. Entrées include steaks, fresh seafood, and chicken. The kids enjoy sipping sarsaparilla and also rummaging through saddlebags for treats and surprises. The restaurant is open for dinner Monday through Thursday from 5:00 to 9:30 P.M.; Friday and Saturday from 5:00 to 10:00 P.M. (with sundown suppers to 5:30 P.M. on those days); on Sundays dinner is served from 4:00 to 9:00 P.M. For reservations call (503) 382–2202. The eatery is located just off Highway 20 in Tumalo, about 4 miles northwest of Bend.

Travelers who hanker for a comfortable out-West experience can check with the friendly folks at **Rock Springs Guest Ranch,** located on 2,500 acres covered with ponderosa pine and juniper, at 64201 Tyler Road, just a short distance from the Tumalo Feed Company. The head wrangler and ranch staff offer horseback riding for the whole family, including special training for youngsters. Two rides are offered every day, with an all-day ride later in the week. On one day you can even ride bareback and test your skills sans saddle if you wish. The weekly package price includes a cozy pine-paneled cabin with a fireplace and delicious meals, all served buffet-style in the main lodge's rustic dining room. Stays run from mid-June to the end of August, Saturday to Saturday, and you're likely to meet folks from all over the United States, Canada, Europe, and even Asia. It's like a great family summer-camp adventure, complete with tons of well-supervised activities for kids. For further information contact the ranch staff at (503) 382–1957.

The community of **Sisters,** transformed into an Old West tourist town with wooden boardwalks and Western-style storefronts, is filled with interesting shops, lovely boutiques, and old-fashioned eateries. Hotel Sisters is one of the few early structures remaining, now restored as an 1880s-style restaurant where you can order chicken-and-dumpling dinners on Sundays. The hotel's colorful saloon looks as though it came right off a western-movie set.

If time allows, detour about 5 miles west of Sisters to see the headwaters of the Metolius River, bubbling directly from the lower north slopes of Black Butte near Camp Sherman. The entire length of the Metolius River offers fishing access, along with campgrounds and river cabins. At the **Wizard Falls Fish Hatchery,** a few miles downriver from Camp Sherman, you can see where those wily trout are raised to stock the more than one hundred lakes in the high Cascades. The Metolius is well known to fly-fishers for its enormous wild trout, and nearby **Lake Billy Chinook,** behind Round Butte Dam, offers some of the best kokanee, or landlocked salmon, troll fishing in the region.

Walk along the ¼-mile **Jack Creek Nature Trail** near Camp Sherman to see native plants and wildflowers thriving in a lush, spring-fed oasis that contrasts with the dry, open forest floor strewn with long pine needles and ponderosa pinecones the size of large baseballs. Peer over the footbridge at Camp Sherman to spot some of the largest trout you've ever laid eyes on, playing hide-and-seek in the clear waters of the Metolius.

If you're looking for a quiet retreat some distance from civilization, consider **Black Butte Ranch,** located just south of the Metolius River headwaters. Nestled on some 1,800 acres of ponderosa pine forest and lovely meadows at the base of 6,436-foot Black Butte—a volcanic cone whose warm innards keep it virtually snow-free all year—the area was, from the late 1800s to about 1969, a working cattle ranch and stopping-off place for sheep and wool coming from eastern Oregon across the Cascade Mountains to the Willamette Valley. Today you can stroll or bicycle along paths that wend around guest quarters, condominiums, and private vacation residences. If you play golf or tennis, you can choose from two 18-hole golf courses and nineteen open-air tennis courts. Or you can paddle a canoe on the small lake just beyond the restaurant and dining room; nestle in front of a friendly fire and watch the squirrels dash about the ponderosa pine just outside a wide expanse of windows; or curl up for a snooze amid the utter quiet in this peaceful spot.

For further information and reservations at Black Butte Ranch during all four seasons, call (503) 595–6211. During winter, you can bring Nordic ski gear and enjoy cross-country treks on those flat meadows, which are covered with snow from November through March.

Just west of Sisters on Highway 126, on the way to Black Butte Ranch, notice a hefty number of woolly llamas in large grassy meadows belonging to the 350-acre Patterson Ranch. Gentle creatures with high intelligence and great curiosity, the llamas are raised here, at one of the largest llama-breeding ranches in North America. You can stop by the roadside to see them.

The Cascade Mountains form an effective weather barrier, with their forested foothills, sparsely clad higher slopes, and snowy volcanic peaks extending down the midsection of the Beaver State and siphoning those heavy rain clouds from the Pacific Ocean to the west. Most of this moisture falls as snow in the high Cascades from November through April, leaving less moisture for the high desert regions east of the mountains. Spring snowmelt gurgles into hundreds of lakes, creeks, and streams, tumbling down the mountainsides to larger rivers that find their way to the Pacific Ocean, completing the eternal cycle.

As they made the first wagon train crossing of the central Cascades south of Bend across Pengra, later renamed **Willamette Pass,** toward Eugene in late fall 1853, those emigrants who crossed the lonely high desert found that the first snows of late autumn had already whitened most of the mountain peaks. With 300 wagons, the half-starved, weary group was nearly stranded in the high country until guided safely to Eugene by resident pioneers who had earlier begun to open the route over the pass.

Years before, around 1826, botanist David Douglas, sent by the British Hudson's Bay Company, trekked through these forests. Early records describe him carrying a pack on his back, a gun across his shoulder and a "shaggy terrier at his heels." Apparently Douglas's skill at shooting birds in flight and magically producing fire from the heavens—by way of a magnifying lens—kept the local Indians "at an admiring distance."

Your visit to the high Cascades wouldn't be complete, however, without including the 87-mile ◆ **Cascades Lakes Scenic Drive,** which meanders along the same routes as the native peoples, botanist Douglas, and explorers like John Frémont, Nathaniel Wyeth, Peter Skene Ogden, and Kit Carson traversed. Designated a National Forest Scenic Byway in 1989, this highway loop from Bend to the **Wickiup Reservoir** was once called Century Drive. In 1920 the original Indian trails, horse trails, and wagon roads were finally replaced by a main wagon road from Bend to Sparks Lake and the Elk Lake area. The new road was similar to the first dirt and gravel road from the Portland area to Government Camp on Mount Hood.

Today you can take the well-paved cinder road to wind your way through ancient lava beds to 6,000-foot **Mt. Bachelor** and down through pine forests, skirting more than a dozen alpine lakes—Sparks, Elk, Big Lava, Little Lava, Cultus, Little Cultus, Deer, North Twin, and South Twin—on whose shores are many campgrounds and places from which to fish. Fly-fishing-only lakes include Davis, Sparks, and Fall River. At Cultus and Little Cultus lakes, an interesting mixture of ponderosa pine, Douglas fir, white fir, white pine, sugar pine, and spruce grows along the road into the lake area; here, too, are some of the few places along the drive that offer shallow sandy beaches.

There are summer hiking and camping areas at most of the lakes, as well as winter cross-country ski trails along the route;

during winter, visitors enjoy skiing into Elk Lake, where rustic **Elk Lake Lodge** remains open year-round. Good sources for maps and information are the Deschutes National Forest Headquarters in Bend and the Central Oregon Recreation Association, P.O. Box 230, Bend 97709 (503–382–8334). Senior day hikes are offered on Wednesdays during summer and fall by the Bend Metro Parks and Recreation Department; for information and current schedules, call (503) 389–PARK.

Because of heavy snowfall in winter and early spring, the Cascade Lakes Scenic Drive is closed past the entrance to the **Mt. Bachelor Ski Area** parking lot from mid-November until late May. You can enjoy driving along this historic route from June through October, accessing it from the north, near Bend, or from the south, near LaPine and the Wickiup Reservoir.

Located just west of Elk Lake and directly south of McKenzie Pass, the 247,000-acre ◆**Three Sisters Wilderness** offers more than 250 miles of trails that skirt alpine meadows, sparkling streams, glittering patches of obsidian, ancient lava flows, old craters, and dozens of small lakes, as well as glaciers at higher elevations. About 40 miles of the **Pacific Crest National Scenic Trail** runs through this vast region, which in the late 1950s was set aside as a wilderness.

Protected by the National Wilderness Preservation Act of 1964, the Three Sisters Wilderness—along with more than 15 million acres of other land so designated across the United States—permits visitors to travel only by foot or by horse—no vehicles are allowed. Oregon has set aside thirteen such wilderness areas, seven of them located from south to north in the Cascade Mountains.

Like the early mountain men, explorers, and naturalists, experienced and well-equipped backpackers will often stay out for four or five days at a time in the high country, letting the wilderness saturate every pore and limb. The Three Sisters Wilderness is accessible from mid-July through October for hiking and from November through June for snow camping and cross-country skiing. Snow often reaches depths of 20 feet or more at the higher elevations, and hikers may encounter white patches up to the first week of August.

Most of the high mountain lakes are stocked with eastern brook, rainbow, and cutthroat trout. From Lava, Elk, and Sparks lakes, you can access trails into the Three Sisters Wilderness, walking just a short distance if time doesn't allow an overnight trek with backpacks and tents.

During summer and fall, you might enjoy seeing the high mountain country on horseback, just as explorers like Lewis and Clark, John Frémont, and Kit Carson did in the early 1800s. The **Metolius-Windigo Trail,** built by horse lovers in cooperation with the Sisters, Bend, and Crescent Ranger District staff, was begun back in the late 1970s and now offers a network of riding trails, as well as campsites with corrals. The Metolius-Windigo Trail runs through the spectacular alpine meadow and high backcountry from Sisters toward Elk Lake and then heads south, following Forest Service roads and sections of the Old Skyline Trail, toward Crescent Lake and Windigo Pass, located off Highway 58, about 60 miles south of Bend.

For horse campers the familiar crackling warmth of a morning fire mixes well with hands that cup mugs of hot coffee before breaking camp and saddling up. The creak of saddle leather punctuates the crisp morning air; the clop of the horses' hooves echoes through the pines; the air smells fresh and clean. Most horse campers are lured by both the wilderness and the simple joys of riding, and many assist hikers in the Adopt-a-Trail program. The Forest Service provides materials and consultation, whereas various hiking and trail-riding groups maintain or build new trails.

For information about guided horseback trips, contact the Sisters Information Center, P.O. Box 476, Sisters 97759 (503–549–0251).

CROOKED RIVER GORGE

About a million years ago, lava spilled into the Crooked River canyon upriver near the community of Terrebonne and flowed nearly to Warm Springs. As you drive though this area, stop at **Peter Skene Ogden Wayside,** just off Highway 97, and peer into a 300-foot-deep rocky chasm where the Crooked River, at its base, is still searching for that old canyon.

If time allows, drive, into the Crooked River Gorge via Highway 27 from Prineville to the large **Prineville Reservoir State Park**—a gorgeous drive into the heart of the gorge and, at its base, the ancient river. There are campgrounds on the lake, which offers fishing throughout the year, including ice fishing in winter. For more information contact the Prineville–Crook County Visitors' Information Center, 390 N. Fairview (P.O. Box 546), Prineville 97754 (503–447–6304). And if you're a rock hound, ask about the annual Thunderegg Days held during midsummer. To access Prineville head east from Redmond for about 20 miles on Highway 126.

Of the nation's nine smokejumper bases, eight are located in the Northwest, and one, **Redmond Smokejumper Base,** is based at the Redmond Air Center, just off Highway 97 and near Redmond. If you call ahead for tour information (503–548–5071), you may get to watch trainees jump from the practice tower in their full smokejumping regalia as well as see how the parachutes and harnesses are repaired, rebuilt, and repacked. Head east via Sisters Avenue, the road out to the Juniper Golf Course, to the airfield's entrance. Note, however, that spring and fall are the best times to arrange a visit; the base may be closed to guests if a summer fire emergency occurs.

Speaking of golf, the **Juniper Golf Club** welcomes all travelers who enjoy the game. Call ahead for a tee time (503–548–3121) for either nine or eighteen holes of golf under a vibrant blue sky and with lush green fairways lined with ponderosa pine, pungent juniper (one of the aromatic cedars), and yellow flowering sagebrush. Wednesday is women's day from 8:00 to 11:00 A.M.; Thursday is men's day from noon to 5:00 P.M. Avid golfing buffs claim that there are more than 216 holes on some fifteen golf courses in the Central Oregon area. For a complete listing contact the Redmond Visitors' Information Center, 427 Southwest Seventh, Redmond 97756. The telephone number is (503) 923–5191.

Then, too, you could detour at Terrebonne, a few miles north of Redmond, and drive out to spectacular **Smith Rock State Park** to watch the rock climbers before heading north on Highway 97 toward the Warm Springs Indian Reservation. The rock climbing at Smith Rock is considered some of the best and most challenging anywhere in the world. As you crane your neck upward to watch the brightly Lycra-clad men and women scale the vertical reddish-colored rock inclines, you may hear words of encouragement in more than a dozen languages—from French, Italian, and German to Swedish, English, and Japanese.

Smith Rock

Free climbing, the most popular form of rock climbing, allows only the use of the rock's natural features to make upward progress; however, safety ropes are allowed to stop a fall. You'll notice climbers on the ascent using just their hands and feet to perch on small outcroppings or to clutch narrow crevices as they carefully negotiate a route to the top; the object is to climb a particular section, or route, "free" without using the safety ropes.

You'll find shady places to picnic here, as well as an easy, ten-minute trail you can walk down to the meandering Crooked River. Then cross the footbridge for a close encounter with those enormous, almost intimidating vertical rocks that nature has painted in shades of deep red-orange, vibrant browns, and pale creams. Be sure to stay a safe distance from the climbers, because loose chunks of rock can dislodge and plummet to the ground.

The best picture-snapping view of Smith Rock and the Crooked River, by the way, is from the far end of the parking area, near the turnaround—an absolute showstopper at sunrise or sunset.

Located in the heart of the Warm Springs Indian Reservation, ◆ **Kah-Nee-Ta Resort** is nestled alongside the Warm Springs River, at the base of another bright copper-and-amber canyon just a few miles from the community of Warm Springs. The moment you turn off Highway 26 and wind down from stark rimrock ridges and sparsely clad hills into the multicolored canyon, city cares will seem far away. The area easily recalls scenes from a well-worn Zane Grey novel or a colorful Charlie Russell painting.

After settling in at Kah-Nee-Ta, one of the best things to do is to lower your travel-weary frame into one of the hot mineral baths in the resort's Village. Follow that leisurely soak with a sweat beneath several layers of sheets and blankets. Yes, sweat. Profusely. You'll emerge cleansed, relaxed, and quite likely a "new person"—the experience is truly one of Kah-Nee-Ta's most memorable offerings.

The resort, owned and operated by the Confederated Indian Tribes of Warm Springs, began welcoming visitors in 1964 with the opening of the Village, which offers comfortable cottages, a number of large teepees for outdoor-style camping, and spaces for recreational vehicles. Three mammoth swimming pools close at hand are fed by the hot mineral springs. On a sagebrush-carpeted bluff just above the Village is the spacious contemporary lodge that opened in 1972. Wrapped around its own jumbo-size pool, the lodge is a good choice if you like your getaways a bit swankier.

For breakfast and lunch enjoy the informal Pinto Coffee Shop or the outdoor patio overlooking the pool; then try the elegant Juniper Room for romantic gourmet dining. An entrée prepared with Cornish game hen called Bird-in-Clay, a house specialty, is worth ordering ahead—notify the dining-room staff about three hours in advance. With its stuffing of wild rice and juniper berries, the dish is delicious.

The charm of Kah-Nee-Ta owes as much to its culture as to its unique rimrock setting. A sense of the Native American past permeates the air, while the unobstructed desert landscape encourages a gentle sifting away of those citified cobwebs. Long walks are a must here—meander down a paved path next to the Warm

Springs River, which bubbles alongside the Village, and catch whiffs of pungent sage, bitterbrush, and juniper.

For further information and reservations, contact the staff at Kah-Nee-Ta, P.O. Box K, Warm Springs 97761 (503–553–1112). The lodge is open year-round, except from mid-November to March; the Village is open all year. The resort is about an hour northwest of the Bend-Redmond-Madras area and two hours east of Portland, via Highway 26 across Mount Hood.

With a massive stone entry shaped like a tribal drum and brick walls fretted with a traditional native basket pattern, the ◆**Museum at Warm Springs** resonates with the cultural past and present of the three Native American tribes—Wasco, Warm Springs, and Paiute—who live in this spectacular rimrock canyon near the Deschutes River. The new museum is one of the premier tribal-owned museums in the United States and visitors can see one of the most extensive collections of Native American artifacts on a reservation. Be sure to stand in the song chamber, where you can hear traditional chanting. Many Indian elders hope that the museum will be an important link to the younger members of the Confederated tribes, teaching them, as well as visitors, about their languages, religions, and cultures. Located just off Highway 97 in Warm Springs, on Shitake Creek, the museum is open from 8:00 A.M. to 5:00 P.M. daily. For further information contact Michael Hammond, museum director, at (503) 553–1161.

PREHISTORIC FOSSIL LANDS

Shaniko, located at the junction of Highways 97 from the Bend-Redmond-Madras area and 218 from the John Day area, was an important shipping point for wheat, wool, and livestock at the turn of the century. The bustling town at the end of the railroad tracks was filled with grain warehouses, corrals, loading chutes, cowboys, sheepherders, hotels, and saloons. Known as the Wool Capital, the town was named for August Scherneckau, whom the Indians called Shaniko and whose ranch house was a station on the old stage route from The Dalles to central Oregon.

The last of the battles between the cattle ranchers and the sheep ranchers were fought near Shaniko in the mid-1850s; for some twenty-five years the former resisted what was considered an invasion of their territory by "those ornery sheepherders."

The sheep won, however, and still dominate the rangelands on the high desert. In fact you should be prepared to wait a considerable amount of time for flocks of the woolly critters to cross various highways throughout the region when the herds are moved to and from mountain pastures in both spring and fall.

Although Shaniko is mostly a ghost town today, a few energetic citizens are breathing new life into the old frontier village. The ♦**Historic Shaniko Hotel,** no longer tired and weather-beaten, has been renovated by Jean Farrell and his wife, Dorothy—transplants from the Salem area. A wide plank porch once again wraps around both sides of the red brick hotel, graceful arched windows sparkle in the morning sun, and oak doors with new glass panels open into a lace-draped, plant-filled lobby that holds one of the original settees and an antique reception desk. The oak banister, refinished and polished, still winds up to the second floor.

Hanging brass plaques also identify sixteen refurbished guest rooms, each named for an early Shaniko pioneer. Shiny brass lamps have replaced bare light bulbs; plush gray carpeting covers floors that earlier sported tired, cracked linoleum; firm mattresses offer rest in place of creaky old springs; lovely linens and floral spreads grace beds that once offered mismatched and worn blankets; and new private bathrooms keep guests from having to trek to the far end of the hall.

What's there to do in Shaniko? Well, mosey over to the gas station and buy a soft drink; capture with a camera or paintbrush the weathered romance of the old school, the jail, and city hall or the water tower and the hotel; peer into old buildings and wonder who lived there; or just sit on the porch swing and reflect about the days when Shaniko bustled with cowboys, ponies, sheepherders, sheep, train whistles, and steam locomotives.

The hotel restaurant, open daily from 7:00 A.M. to 10:00 P.M., serves moderately priced meals. For further information and reservations, contact the Farrells and their staff at the Historic Shaniko Hotel, Shaniko 97057 (503–489–3415).

With luck you refilled your picnic basket and cooler in Bend, Redmond, or Madras before heading to Shaniko and can now continue east on Highway 218 for about 20 miles, driving into the ♦**John Day Fossil Beds National Monument** area. Stop to see the Palisades of the **Clarno Unit,** just east of the John Day

Old farmhouse near Shaniko

River. Not only the leaves but also the limbs, seeds, and nuts of the tropical plants that grew here 40 to 50 million years ago are preserved in the oldest of the Cenozoic era's layers, the Clarno formation, named for Andrew Clarno, an early white settler who homesteaded here in 1866. The formation is a mudflow conglomerate that has been battered by eons of weather; you'll notice the unusual leftovers—eroded pillars, craggy turrets, top-heavy pedestals, natural stone bridges, and deep chasms. Walk up the slope from the picnic area to stand amid these intriguing shapes and notice pungent-smelling sagebrush and junipers dotting the otherwise-barren hills where a tropical forest once grew. *Note:* There's not water here, and although they usually hide in rock crevices, keep an eye out for the Western Pacific rattlesnake while you're in the area.

According to analysis of the bone and plant fossils unearthed here, first by a cavalry officer and then by Thomas Condon, a minister and amateur paleontologist who settled in The Dalles in the 1850s, an ancient lush tropical forest contained palm, fig, cinnamon, hydrangea, sequoia, and ferns, together with alligators, primitive rhinoceroses, and tiny four-footed horses. As you walk along the interpretive **Trail of the Fossils,** notice the many leaf prints in which every vein and tooth has been preserved in the chalky-colored hardened clays.

When Condon first learned of the area, through specimens brought to The Dalles, he explored it and found other hidden clues to Oregon's past. In 1870 he shipped a collection of fossil teeth to Yale University, and during the next thirty years many of the world's leading paleontologists came to Oregon to study the John Day fossil beds. Three large units in the region, encompassing more than 14,000 acres, were designated a national monument in 1974 and are now under the direction of the National Park Service. The digging and collecting of fossil materials are coordinated by two Park Service paleontologists, and evidence of new species of prehistoric mammals continues to surface as the ancient layers of mud, ash, and rock are washed and blown away by rain and wind each year. The Hancock Field Station, located on the Clarno Unit and near the small community of Fossil and the John Day River, offers outdoor workshops and fossil-hunting field trips for kids of all ages during the summer; you can obtain information from the Oregon Museum of Science and Industry in Portland by calling (503) 797–4000.

If you discover some interesting fossil remains while exploring the area, the park staff encourages reporting their locations so that the findings can be identified and cataloged into the computer.

To visit the **Painted Hills** Unit, continue on Highway 218 to Fossil, head south past Shelton Wayside and Campground—a lovely oasis and a good picnic spot—and turn onto Highway 207 toward Mitchell, a total of about 60 miles. Find the turnoff to the Painted Hills just a few miles west, then continue 6 miles north to the viewpoint.

The vast array of cone-shaped hills is actually layer upon layer of volcanic ash from those huge mountains such as Newberry and Mazama that each collapsed in a fiery roar thousands of years ago. Some of the layers of tuff are stained a rich maroon or pink, others are yellow-gold, and still others are black or bronze. The colors are muted by late afternoon's golden light and at sunset turn a deep burgundy. As you behold this barren, surrealistic landscape, you'll blink and wonder whether you aren't really looking at a marvelous watercolor or oil painting.

For a closer view of the brilliantly colored bands of tuff, walk along the ½-mile trail from the overlook, or drive to nearby **Painted Cove Trail.** *Note:* Remember to take drinking water into both the Clarno and the Painted Hills units.

Later, returning to Mitchell, you might plan a coffee break at the **Blueberry Muffin Cafe,** located right on Highway 26. Here friendly conversation is offered along with breakfast, lunch, and dinner. The cafe is open Monday through Saturday from 6:30 A.M. to 7:00 P.M. and Sunday from 7:00 A.M. to 7:00 P.M.; the phone number is (503) 462–3434.

Continuing east about 30 miles, stop at **Picture Gorge** before turning north on Highway 19 for a couple of miles to the Cant Ranch Visitors' Center. At Picture Gorge you can easily see the oldest to youngest major formations, all marching across the landscape in orderly layers of mud, ash, and rock—the Picture Gorge Basalt, about 15 million years old; Mascall Formation, about 12 million years old; and the narrow ridge on top, named the Rattlesnake Formation, about 3 million years old. You can discern where the two oldest formations were tilted southward together and eroded before the rattlesnake formation was laid down across them, horizontally. Another good place to see the rattlesnake layer, the narrow rimrock at the top of most canyons, is on your drive down into the Warm Springs Canyon and into the tribal village of Warm Springs, before the turnoff to Kah-Nee-Ta Resort.

Plan a stop at the **Cant Ranch** Visitors' Center, where fossil replicas and actual specimens from the three units are displayed and identified. You can also watch park staff prepare the fossils for exhibiting, and you can ask questions about the specimens you find and report. In the orchard nearby a collection of farm implements from the ranch is being restored, and in the main ranch house one of the rooms has been set aside to look just as it did some sixty years ago, complete with original furnishings and an arrangement of Cant family photos. The visitors' center is open from about mid-March through October from 9:00 A.M. to 6:00 P.M. Drinking water is available at Cant Ranch and also at the Foree Deposit area in the nearby **Sheep Rock Unit**; both facilities are also wheelchair-accessible. Additional information and maps are available from the John Day

Fossil Beds National Monument headquarters, 420 W. Main Street, John Day 97845 (503–575–0721).

Campgrounds in the area include those at **Shelton Wayside State Park;** the Clyde Holiday Wayside on Highway 26 near Mt. Vernon about 30 miles east of the Cant Ranch Visitors' Center; and the primitive camping areas in the **Strawberry Mountain Wilderness** south of John Day and Canyon City. Current camping information is also posted in each unit of the park.

There are a limited number of motels and restaurants in Mount Vernon and Mitchell; more can be found in Prineville or in John Day, about 5 miles east of Mt. Vernon. For current information contact the Grant County Visitors' Information Center, 281 W. Main Street, John Day 97845 (503–575–0547).

If you head west from Mitchell toward Prineville and Redmond, completing the western loop into high desert fossil country, plan to picnic or camp at **Ochoco Lake State Park,** just on the western edge of the **Ochoco National Forest.** An interesting side trek is the 10-mile drive on mostly gravel-surfaced Forest Service road to see **Stein's Pillar.** The basalt pillar rises some 250 feet from the forest floor, ancient layers of clay jutting into the deep blue sky. For information about hiking and camping in the area, contact the Ochoco National Forest, P.O. Box 155, Prineville 97754 (503–447–6247). Access the road to Stein's Pillar just across the highway from the Ochoco Lake State Park turnoff.

For information about motel accommodations, contact the Prineville–Crook County Visitors' Information Center, 390 North Fairview, Prineville 97754. The telephone number is (503) 447–6304.

Rugged Hells Canyon

As you head east from Mitchell and the Cant Ranch Visitors' Center, Highway 26 meanders into the **John Day Valley,** where vast cattle ranches spread to the east and where yellow pine is logged in the Malheur National Forest to the south and north. Native peoples roamed for thousands of years in this region, hunting in the same mountains and fishing the rivers and streams. Many features in the area were named for John Day, the Virginia pioneer, explorer, and trapper who in 1812 traveled through the area with the Overland Expedition of the Pacific Fur

Company, on his way to the mouth of the Columbia River and the new fur-trading settlement of Astoria.

At the **Grant County Museum** in nearby Canyon City, you'll see an old jail from a nearby ghost town—Greenhorn, located just northeast of John Day—and a cabin that reportedly once belonged to poet Joaquin Miller. In its heyday Canyon City bulged with more than 10,000 miners and gold prospectors; gold was discovered here in 1862 by several miners who were on their way to the goldfields in Idaho. The placers of Whiskey Gulch, Canyon Creek, and other nearby streams produced several million dollars' worth of the gold stuff before the turn of the century. The historical museum, located at 101 S. Canyon Boulevard–Highway 395, is open June through September from 9:30 A.M. to 4:30 P.M., Monday–Saturday, and from 1:00 to 5:00 P.M. on Sundays.

Highway 26 winds east and north from John Day into the Malheur National Forest, over 5,280-foot Dixie Pass toward Sumpter and Baker City. You can detour at Sumpter for a nostalgic train ride on the ◆**Sumpter Valley Narrow Gauge Railroad.** Board the train at the Sumpter Valley Railroad Park; then ride behind a puffing, wood-burning 1914 Heisler steam locomotive, *Stumpdodger,* through the forested valley etched with dredge tailings. The old train once transported gold ore and logs from the hard-rock mountain mines and pine-dotted Sumpter Valley. During the hour-long ride, watch for geese, heron, beaver, deer, and coyotes—and an occasional raid by "honest-to-goodness train robbers." The train runs weekends through the summer and into September.

A live ghost town, Sumpter contains about 140 residents, three restaurants, two stores, and a restored circa 1900 church and offers visitors a summer celebration, a winter snowmobile festival, and more than 200 miles of cross-country ski trails. While eating at the **Sumpter Nugget** or at the **Elkhorn Saloon and Cafe,** you'll most likely encounter one of those old prospectors and hear a yarn or two about the 1800s gold rush days and how the town was destroyed by fire in 1917.

To explore the area on your own, get a copy of the **Elkhorn National Forest Scenic Byway** map, which is packed with helpful information and photographs. This self-guided summertime drive takes you along the 100-mile Sumpter Valley loop, where you can see old mines, abandoned mine shafts, and even a ghost town or two. If you're a ghost-town buff, visit the remains of two towns along the route, Bourne and Granite. Such characters as Skedaddle Smith, One-eyed Dick, and '49 Jimmie reportedly lived in Granite in the old days.

Call innkeeper Joy Myers at **Sumpter Bed and Breakfast** (503–894–2229) and plan to stay overnight at her cozy four-guest-room inn that dates back to the turn of the century. This way you can fully immerse yourself in gold mining history and, perhaps, even spot the "ghost locomotive," a phantom of old logging and mining days that folks occasionally say they spy hiding along the Middle Fork of the John Day River. Other ghost towns in the area include Greenhorn, Susanville, and Whitney.

You can obtain a copy of the Elkhorn National Forest Scenic Byway map from the Baker Ranger District, Route 1, Box 1, Baker City 97814, or call Wallowa-Whitman National Forest headquarters in Baker City at (503) 523–6391. Further information about Sumpter, the *Stumpdodger* train schedule, and about the restoration of the Sumpter Dredge can be obtained from the Baker County Visitors' Information Center, 490 Campbell Street, Baker City 07814, or call (503) 523–5855.

The settlement of Baker City grew up around a mill built in the 1860s by J. W. Virtue to process ore brought from those first hard-rock gold mines. By 1890 the town had grown to nearly 6,700, larger than any city in the eastern section of the state, and a fledgling timber industry had been started by David Eccles, who also was founder of the Sumpter Valley Railroad. When mining declined after World War I, loggers, cattle herders, and ranchers replaced those colorful miners and gold prospectors.

The **Baker City Historic District** includes about sixty-four early buildings, some constructed from volcanic tuff and stone. Also worth a visit is the **Historical Cemetery,** located near the high school. For both attractions pick up the self-guided walking-tour map at the visitors' center. And plan a visit, too, to the U.S. National Bank, at 2000 Main Street, where you'll see a whopping, 80.4-ounce gold nugget that was found in the area during the early gold rush days.

Located just a few blocks north of the visitors' center, at the corner of Campbell and Grove streets, is the **Oregon Trail Regional Museum,** featuring a collection of pioneer artifacts gathered from the Old Oregon Trail. Often such prized possessions as trunks, furniture, china, silver, and glassware were left along the trail in order to lighten the wagons for the starving and exhausted oxen or horses. The kids will enjoy the historic gold mining exhibits, an impressive gem and mineral collection, and regional Native American baskets, arrowheads, tools, and clothing. The museum is open daily from 10:00 A.M. to 1:00 P.M. but is closed during winter months; its phone number is (503) 523–9308.

From Baker City detour about 5 miles east on Highway 86 to Flagstaff Summit to visit the impressive and new **National Historic Oregon Trail Interpretive Center.** This panoramic site overlooks miles of the original wagon trail ruts that have, over the last 150 years since the 1840s and 1850s, receded gently into the sagebrush- and bitterbrush-littered landscape. Now the ruts are just dim outlines, reminders of the pioneer past, and eyes squint to follow the old trail across the wide desert toward the Blue Mountains, a low, snow-dusted range that hovers on the far northwestern horizon.

In the main gallery of the 23,000-square-foot center, more than 300 photographs, drawings, paintings, and maps depict the toil, sweat, and hardships of the 2,000-mile journey from Independence, Missouri, to Oregon City and the lush Willamette Valley located south of the Portland area. Not just a collection of dusty artifacts housed behind glass, the exhibits are "hands-on"; kids as well as oldsters are encouraged to hug the buffalo, pile gear into an miniature wagon, and pan for gold in an outdoor living-history exhibit. You can attend special programs in the outdoor Amphitheater, stroll the living-history pioneer encampment, and walk some of the 4.2 miles of interpretive trails. The Main Loop Trail to and from Panorama Point and around a section of those original wagon ruts takes about two hours. *Note:* Stay on the trail and be alert for ticks, scorpions, and rattlesnakes during the hot summer months when temperatures often exceed 100 degrees. The elevation is about 3,700 feet.

For brochures, maps, and other information, contact the Bureau of Land Management, P.O. Box 987, Baker City 97814. The telephone number is (503) 523–1843. Many volunteers assist the Oregon Trail Center staff, and you can get involved, too, in bringing history alive at Flagstaff Hill. The Interpretive Center is open May 1 through September 30 from 9:00 A.M. to 6:00 P.M. daily and October 1 through April 30 to 4:00 P.M. daily. Admission is free.

While the Oregon Trail left the Snake River at Farewell Bend, south of Baker City toward Ontario, and continued northwest into Baker Valley and over the Blue Mountains toward The Dalles, the ancient river headed directly north, chiseling and sculpting **Hells Canyon**—a spectacular, 6,000-foot-deep fissure between high craggy mountains. To experience this awesome chunk of geography that separates Oregon and Idaho and is the deepest river gorge in the world, head east to Halfway via Highway 86 from Flagstaff Summit.

Included in this vast region are the 108,000-acre **Hells Canyon Wilderness,** the 662,000-acre **Hells Canyon National Recreation Area,** and the **Wild and Scenic Snake River Corridor.** Visit the canyon during spring or early autumn, when native shrubs, trees, and flowers are at their best; summers are quite hot and dry. If possible, take one of the float or jet-boat trips on the river or, if you're in good shape, a guided backpack or horseback trip into the wilderness areas. For helpful information contact the Oregon Guides and Packers Association, P.O. Box 3797, Portland 97208 (503–234–2173).

If you're interested in fall hunting in the region, contact the Oregon Hunter's Association, Baker County Chapter, at (503) 523–6561. Try lovely Hewitt Park and the 50-mile Brownlee Reservoir for picnicking, fishing, and camping on the waters of the Snake River behind Brownlee Dam, just south of Halfway.

You might want to refill your picnic basket and cooler in Halfway and take the narrow road that winds from Oxbow Dam along a 23-mile scenic stretch of the Snake River down to Hells Canyon Dam spillway and one of the jet-boat launch areas. There is a portable rest room here and a visitors' information trailer, but no other services. In late spring you'll see masses of yellow lupine, yellow and gold daisies, and pink wild roses blooming among crevices in craggy basalt bluffs and outcroppings that hover over the narrow roadway. It's well worth the 46-mile round-trip to experience this accessible section of the ◆**Hells Canyon National Recreation Area.** You could enjoy your picnic at the boat-launch site, or return to Hells Canyon Park, located about halfway back to Highway 86. The park offers picnic areas, comfortable grassy places to sit, and a boat launch, all next to the river. Overnight campsites are available at Copperfield Park, located on this scenic drive about 17 miles from Halfway.

Further information can be obtained from Hells Canyon National Recreation Area, 88401 Highway 82, Enterprise 97828 (503–426–4978) or from the Wallowa-Whitman National Forest headquarters in Baker City (503–523–6391).

THE HIGH WALLOWAS

Heading north from Baker City toward LaGrande, take old Highway 30 instead of Interstate 84 and detour at Haines to eat at one of the best and most well-known restaurants in the northeastern section of the state, **Haines Steak House.** Owners Steve and Gail Hart remodeled the old structure after a fire, filling it once again with western cowboy memorabilia and offering the old-fashioned hospitality so typical of this region. After the salad bar you'll work your way through a bowl of hearty soup, western-style baked beans, and a delicious charcoal-grilled steak fresh off the rangelands. The restaurant, open for dinner Wednesday through Monday, is on Old Highway 30 in Haines, about 10 miles north of Baker City; the phone number is (503) 856–3639.

If you pass through this region of the Beaver State in mid-spring, say, late May, continue from Haines on Highway 237, ignoring Interstate 84 for a while longer, and drive slowly through the small community of Union. Here pause to feast your eyes on a number of enormous lilac trees in full, glorious bloom. Many of the lilacs here were brought across the Oregon Trail in the 1840s, "starts" from beloved plants growing at former homes and homesteads back East. Also look for wild iris that bloom profusely in pastures and fields between North Powder and Union.

You could decide to stay over in LaGrande, just a few miles northwest of Union via Highway 203, a good-size town with many restaurants, shops, and services. If you do, call innkeepers Marjorie and Pat McClure at **Stang Manor Inn.** In this spacious Georgian Colonial mansion, built in the 1920s by an early lumber baron, you can rest in elegant comfort surrounded by lovely grounds in which are growing several large lilac trees and a collection of old roses. The McClures are continuing the bed-and-breakfast tradition begun by Steve and Gail Hart, who initiated the restoration of the 10,000-square-foot mansion in the late 1980s. For information and reservations contact the innkeepers at 1612 Walnut Street, LaGrande 97850. The telephone number is (503) 963–9152.

Next, drive from LaGrande into Enterprise and Joseph to treat yourself to a ride on the ◆ **Wallowa Lake Tramway.** Snuggling with three other mountain lovers in a small, open-air gondola, you'll ascend safely to the top of 8,200-foot Mt. Howard for some of the most breathtaking views in the entire region. More than a mile below, Wallowa Lake shimmers in the afternoon sun, reaching into the **Eagle Cap Wilderness** and mirroring eight other snowcapped peaks. To the east lie the rugged canyons of the Imnaha and Snake rivers. As one soaks in the alpine vastness of it all, it's easy to understand why Chief Joseph and his Nez Percé tribe fought to remain in this beautiful area in the mid-1800s when the first white settlers began to encroach on their historic territory. At the top of the tramway are short trails for hiking and a snack shop for obtaining cold drinks or cups of hot coffee before you head back down the mountain.

Access the Enterprise-Joseph area from LaGrande, via Interstate 84 from Haines, heading north on Highway 82. You'll travel about 65 miles to Enterprise, 6 miles farther to Joseph, and another 6 miles to **Wallowa Lake Lodge** and the tramway. The Wallowa Lake area opens for the summer season on Memorial Day weekend; winter visits offer miles of cross-country ski trails through a snowy wonderland.

If the notion of packing your tent and camping beneath tall alpine fir at the edge of a mountain lake sounds inviting, consider making a reservation at the Wallowa State Park campground; the phone number is (503) 432–4185. Be sure to call sometime in midspring, before all the spaces are taken, because everyone else likes to go off the beaten path here as well. For reservations at Wallowa Lake Lodge, perched at the south end of the lake since 1923 and recently renovated, contact the staff at Route 1, Box 320, Joseph 97846 (503–432–9821). In the refurbished dining room, you can sit at a table overlooking the lake and enjoy delicious entrées from farms, fields, and streams throughout the Northwest. The lodge and restaurant are open from May 1 until the snow flies, around November 1, though plans are underway to operate year-round.

For a pleasant overnight bed-and-breakfast experience, call the friendly innkeepers at ◆ **Bed, Bread & Trail Inn** in the small community of Joseph. The couple offers five lovely guest rooms, scrumptious breakfasts, and lots of helpful information about

Wallowa Lake Tramway

what to see and do in the Wallowa Lake area. The telephone number is (503) 432–9765.

One such excursion is a visit to the ♦**Valley Bronze Foundry,** which offers tours year-round, although schedules may vary. On the two-hour tour, you'll get to see the labor-intensive bronze-making process, including the "lost wax process," the production method the business has used since it began operation with a handful of workers in 1982. Many elegant bronze sculptures are on display, some of which are destined for places as far away as Berlin, Germany. For further details phone the staff at (503) 432–7235. Additional information about the area can be obtained from the Joseph Visitors' Information Center, P.O. Box 13, Joseph 97846. The telephone number is (503) 432–1015.

Further information about the area can be obtained from the Wallowa County Visitors Information Center, P.O. Box 427, Enterprise 97828 (503–426–4622). For maps and information about camping and hiking in the Wallowa Mountains and Eagle Cap Wilderness, contact the Wallowa-Whitman National Forest headquarters, P.O. Box 907, Baker 97814 (503–523–6391).

Heading back to LaGrande and busy Interstate 84, where you'll again be following the Oregon Trail wagon route across the Blue Mountains, you can also stop to visit pioneer displays at both **Hilgard Junction** Campground, near LaGrande, and **Emigrant Springs State Park,** about halfway to Pendleton. Emigrant Springs has hookups for recreational vehicles.

Although the four seasons come and go in the nearby Walla Walla Valley, the ♦**Frazier Farmstead Museum and Gardens,** at the south end of Milton-Freewater, seems preserved in time, resembling a slice of small-town America at the turn of the century. The six-acre farmstead, with its large, white, circa 1892 house, gardens, and outbuildings, is located near downtown Walla Walla. William Samuel Frazier and his wife, Rachel Paulina, first bought a 320-acre land claim here, near the Walla Walla River, and built a cabin in 1868.

The family, including seven children, left Texas in the early spring of 1867 in three wagons and arrived in the valley at the base of the Blue Mountains in late autumn of that year. A plain pine secretary desk transported in one of the wagons is one of the prized pieces you can see in the house. When the farmstead was willed to the Milton-Freewater Area Foundation in 1978, to be maintained as a museum, volunteers from the local historical society cataloged more than 700 items and memorabilia, including vintage farm equipment, old photographs, heirloom linens, and family letters from the Civil War.

The well-kept farmstead is a prime example of the community-based preservation movement that began in the mid-1970s during the nation's bicentennial. "The family left all their possessions in the barns and in the house, so we were able to preserve everything," explains Diane Biggs, the museum's curator and an avid horticulturist. "The foundation leased the property to the Milton-Freewater Area Historical Society, and everyone rolled up their sleeves and donated countless hours to the restoration—the farmstead museum opened officially on October 6, 1984."

Working as hard in the beautiful flower and vegetable garden as in the house, Diane sets out hundreds of annuals, herbs, and perennials early each spring. Harvested in late summer and fall, the lush flowers and plants provide bouquets, herbs, and dried flowers sold at the annual **Frazier Farmstead Festival,** held on the first Saturday of October. If you're fortunate enough to be in the area that weekend, you can watch demonstrations of old pioneer crafts and skills, munch an authentic farm-country lunch, and buy homemade preserves, herbal vinegars, and voluminous bouquets. The Frazier Farmstead Museum, located at 1403 Chestnut Street in Milton-Freewater (503–938–4636 or 503–938–3480), is open April through December; visitors are welcome Thursday through Saturday from 11:00 A.M. to 4:00 P.M. and Sunday from 1:00 to 4:00 P.M.

For a close-up experience with the not-too-distant past, pause in Pendleton to trek back in time to one of the city's unusual historical places, the **Pendleton Underground.** You'll walk through a section of the underground where scores of Chinese laborers lived during the early days of this wild West town. Because of the negative feelings against those of Asian backgrounds, the men rarely came above these dimly lit caverns except to work on the construction of the railroad; even their own businesses and services were located in the underground tunnels. The guided tour starts from the Shamrock Cardroom, 37 SW Emigrant Street, one of the wild-and-woolly honky-tonks that flourished in the early 1900s. Tours run at intervals between

9:30 A.M. and 4:00 P.M., and reservations are recommended; call Pam McKay at (503) 276–0730. Ask, too, about the Cozy Rooms Bordello tour. For overnight accommodations with a historic flavor, try Pam's hostelry, **Working Girls Old Hotel Bed and Breakfast,** located at 17 SW Emigrant Street, which also uses the bordello theme in its decor: old brick walls, 18-foot-high ceilings, and baths "down the hall." For information use the same telephone number, (503) 276–0730. For eateries try Cimmiyotti's on Main Street, Crabby's Underground Saloon & Dance Hall on First Street, or Raphael's on Fourth Street. Further information can be obtained from the the Pendleton–Umatilla County Visitors' Information Center, 25 SE Dorion Street, Pendleton 97801. The telephone number is (503) 276–7411 or (800) 547–8911.

Portland and Environs

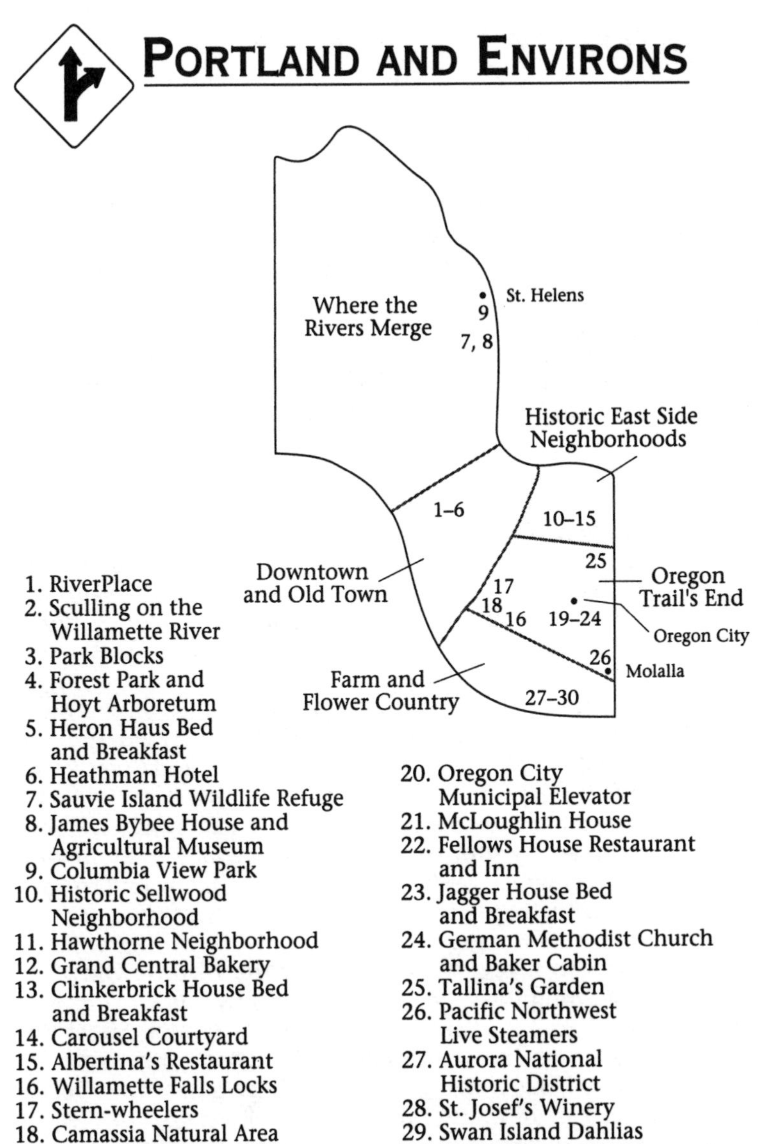

1. RiverPlace
2. Sculling on the Willamette River
3. Park Blocks
4. Forest Park and Hoyt Arboretum
5. Heron Haus Bed and Breakfast
6. Heathman Hotel
7. Sauvie Island Wildlife Refuge
8. James Bybee House and Agricultural Museum
9. Columbia View Park
10. Historic Sellwood Neighborhood
11. Hawthorne Neighborhood
12. Grand Central Bakery
13. Clinkerbrick House Bed and Breakfast
14. Carousel Courtyard
15. Albertina's Restaurant
16. Willamette Falls Locks
17. Stern-wheelers
18. Camassia Natural Area
19. End of the Oregon Trail Interpretive Center
20. Oregon City Municipal Elevator
21. McLoughlin House
22. Fellows House Restaurant and Inn
23. Jagger House Bed and Breakfast
24. German Methodist Church and Baker Cabin
25. Tallina's Garden
26. Pacific Northwest Live Steamers
27. Aurora National Historic District
28. St. Josef's Winery
29. Swan Island Dahlias
30. Canby Depot Museum and Clackamas County Fair

PORTLAND AND ENVIRONS

DOWNTOWN AND OLD TOWN

In the late 1840s Portland was a small clump of log cabins on the banks of the Willamette River, where riverboats laden with people and supplies scuttled back and forth between Fort Vancouver and Oregon City, some 20 miles upriver. Early settlers chopped down stands of tall Douglas fir along the riverbanks to make room for those first small cabins, and the place was called The Clearing. Later the tree stumps were whitewashed to prevent folks from stumbling over them after dark, and the nickname Stumptown emerged.

During the 1850s and 1860s, steamboats appeared, and Stumptown emerged a full-fledged town with a new name decided by the toss of a coin. Now, a century and a half later, the greater Portland area is a large region containing three of the most populated counties in the state—Multnomah, Washington, and Clackamas—and offering visitors a variety of mountains and rivers, vineyards and wineries, museums and historic sites, and contemporary homes and vintage farms, as well as theaters, zoos, festivals, and unique shops, eateries, and hostelries.

The city proper is now situated on both sides of the broad **Willamette River,** stretching east toward Mt. Hood and west into the Tualatin Hills toward the Tualatin Valley and Coast Range. The Willamette flows into the mighty Columbia River just a few miles northwest of the downtown area. The whitewashed stumps long gone, today's visitor will find broad avenues and fountains, parks and lovely public gardens, and, of course, many bridges spanning the Willamette to connect the east and west sides of town.

One of the best ways to get acquainted with the Beaver State's largest city is to take a walking tour of the Historic Old Town area, where Stumptown began. First, stop by the Greater Portland Visitors' Information Center at 26 SW Salmon Street, just across from **Waterfront Park,** for helpful brochures and maps. Then slip into your walking shoes and head across the street to the paved esplanade along the Willamette River.

For a shoreside view of the river, first while away an hour or so at ◆ **RiverPlace,** located on the west riverbank near the heart of the downtown area. It contains condominiums and offices, restaurants—one of them right on the water—and delis, gift shops and boutiques, the European-style **Alexis Hotel,** and a large boat marina. There are comfortable benches for sitting and watching myriad activities, both on the water and ashore. On blue-sky days, lunching at one of the round tables outdoors is one of the most pleasant downtown options.

On almost any day you can see energetic members of the Portland Rowing Club ◆ **sculling on the river** in sleek shells that hold from two to four rowers; one of the best times to watch, though, is at 5:00 A.M., when some of the most devoted rowers scull across the river's early morning, glasslike surface. When the group formed in 1879, it was called the Portland Rowing Association; by 1891, the North Pacific Association of Amateur Oarsmen had been established by active rowing clubs in Portland and as far away as Vancouver, British Columbia, and Coeur d'Alene, Idaho.

World War II brought an end to rowing in Portland for about thirty years, until the early 1970s, when a group of former college oarsmen organized a group called Station L, composed of master oarsmen and college-club crews from both Reed College and Lewis and Clark College. Given the former dusty, leaking boathouse and empty racks, the sport in Portland has come far—the spiffy new racing shells have found not only a permanent home on the new docks at RiverPlace but many ardent participants and enthusiastic spectators as well.

Two women's crews from the Portland Rowing Club won national championships in Seattle in 1986, and rowers now congregate from all over the Northwest to compete in the annual Portland Regatta in mid-April. At this event, both men and women vie for the racing cups and there are competitions for juniors as well.

You can watch the races from RiverPlace Marina or from the grassy sloping lawn at **Tom McCall Waterfront Park,** just next to the Alexis Hotel. Following the races there's usually a water-ski extravaganza that features barefoot waterskiing, ski jumping, human pyramids, swivel-ski ballets, and adagio doubles. All in all, the goings-on make for a fun day on the historic Willamette River, where Stumptown began. If you'd like to explore learning to row the sleek racing shells yourself, stop for information at the Rowing Shop, near the marina shops and delis.

To continue your walking tour, head north from RiverPlace and Waterfront Park on the esplanade along the seawall. During Portland's annual **Rose Festival,** held the first three weeks in June, the seawall is filled with ships of all sizes and lengths, heralding from U.S. Navy and Coast Guard as well as Canadian ports, and many can be toured during the festival. At SW Ankeny and First avenues, stop to see the **Skidmore Fountain,** one of the city's first public fountains. It was donated by a local druggist "for the benefit of the horses, men, and dogs of Portland." **New Market Theatre,** at 50 SW Second Street, is now full of specialty shops but was built in 1872 as both a market and a theater—sopranos sang arias on the second floor while merchants sold cabbages on the first. And at the north end of the Central Fire Station is a small museum devoted to fire fighting and containing vintage fire engines; find it just across from Ankeny Park and the Skidmore Fountain.

At the **Architectural Preservation Gallery,** on NE Second and Couch streets, you can see changing exhibits of historic building fragments, paintings, and old photographs; you can also visit the **Portland Police Museum,** housed in the same site. The Pioneer Courthouse, at SW Fifth and Yamhill, was built in 1869, making it the oldest public building in the Pacific Northwest. Just across the street from the courthouse, detour through **Pioneer Square,** an enormous, block-wide square almost in the heart of the city; colorful outdoor events are held here throughout the year.

The ◆ **Park Blocks,** constructed on land set aside in 1852 for a city park, stretch from SW Salmon Street south, and slightly uphill to the **Oregon Historical Center,** the **Portland Art Museum,** and the campus of **Portland State University.** Here you'll find shady places to walk, rest, and watch the pigeons, and you may well encounter roving musicians or street performers from such local theater groups as Artists Repertory, New Rose, Storefront, and Firehouse, along with the ever-present college students, museum-goers, and people watchers.

The Oregon Historical Center, at 1230 SW Park Avenue, comprises a fine museum of changing exhibits, a historical research library, a gift shop, and a bookstore. The center is open Monday through Saturday, from 10:00 A.M. to 4:45 P.M.; its phone number is (503) 222–1741.

Located directly across Park Blocks from the Historical Center, the Art Museum contains an excellent permanent exhibit of Northwest Coast Indian art and artifacts; museum and gallery lovers can also inquire here about the numerous small galleries sprinkled throughout the downtown area. If you're in the area in late fall, when the tall, leafy trees in the Park Blocks are ablaze with bright yellow, orange, and red autumn hues, consider attending one of the **Wednesday Evening Jazz Concerts** held in the indoor sculpture court at the Art Museum; the concert program starts around the third week in October. The museum is open Tuesday through Thursday from 11:00 A.M. to 7:00 P.M., Friday from 11:00 A.M. to 9:30 P.M., and Saturday and Sunday from noon to 5:00 P.M. For more information call the museum at (503) 226–2811.

For an impromptu snack in the Park Blocks, pick up picnic fixings at **Metro on Broadway,** near Broadway and Salmon Street, just a couple of blocks south of Pioneer Square, or at the **Heathman Bakery and Deli,** on Ninth and Salmon streets, (503–227–5700). Should you walk through the downtown area on a weekend, stop by the colorful **Saturday Market,** situated under the west end of the Burnside Bridge, just north of the Skidmore Fountain. Here you can stroll through a variety of booths that offer a handsome array of Oregon and Pacific Northwest goods, from pottery, wood, and leather to jewelry, candles, and handwoven items. Jugglers and musicians entertain, and from open-air food stands you can choose tasty, ready-to-eat meat and veggie items.

If you're ready to leave the bustle of downtown and enjoy a lazy afternoon in the outdoors, visit cool, shady **Forest Park,** one of the largest urban parks in the United States. All 4,700 acres of the park begin just a few blocks from the Willamette River, off West Burnside Street and adjacent to **Washington Park International Rose Test Gardens** and the gorgeous **Japanese Garden.** The easy Wildwood Trail can be accessed either near the Japanese Garden or from the World Forestry Center, near the Portland Metropolitan Zoo, just west of Washington Park.

Along 10 miles of trails in nearby **Hoyt Arboretum,** you can try your hand at identifying Douglas fir, Jeffrey pine, broadleaved maple, hemlock, red cedar, and grand fir, as well as cherry, ash, madrona, and Indian plum. Spectacular in the spring are native wildflowers, including trillium and buttercups. More than

110 different species of birds and more than 50 species of animals have been identified in Forest Park and the arboretum.

Pick up trail maps and informational literature at Tree House, located at 4000 SW Fairview Boulevard (503–228–4492). Ask about guided tours through the 175-acre arboretum, which contains some 600 species of trees from all over the world. Information about other guided tours, nature walks, and interesting day trips in the area can also be obtained from the staff at the Parks and Recreation office, 1120 SW Fifth Avenue, Room 502 (503–796–5132) and from the Metro Regional Parks and Greenspaces Department, 600 Northeast Grand Avenue, Portland 97232 (503–797–1850). Ask for a copy of the brochure *Trip Into Nature.*

After a busy day of exploring, you can arrange an overnight stay at one of the many comfortable inns or small hotels in the city. One of the newer inns is ◆**Heron Haus Bed and Breakfast,** located in the northwest hills near Washington Park. Its entire back side layered with a lush growth of ivy, the elegant Tudor-style mansion looks very much like one that belongs on a sorority or fraternity row. On the second and third floors are six spacious guest rooms with comfortable sitting spaces, cozy pillows, a plethora of books and magazines, and private baths. One suite features a romantic whirlpool spa, where a couple can relax in bubbly comfort and see a myriad of city lights far below. A light continental breakfast is served in the fireplace dining room, or, on sunny mornings, perhaps in the enclosed sun porch overlooking the pool, the city, and Mount Hood to the east.

The inn is also close to Washington Park Rose gardens, the Japanese Garden, and an assortment of interesting northwest Portland shops, boutiques, and eateries that range along Twenty-first and Twenty-third avenues just north of Burnside Street. For information and reservations contact innkeeper Julie Keppeler at Heron Haus, 2545 NW Westover Road, Portland 97210. The telephone number is (503) 274–1846 .

One of the most charming hostelries right in the heart of the downtown area, just up Broadway from Pioneer Square, is the ◆**Heathman Hotel.** It's also conveniently located next door to the **Arlene Schnitzer Concert Hall,** the **Performing Arts Center,** and the South Park Blocks. Making its debut in the jazzy 1920s, the Heathman served Portlanders and travelers for nearly fifty years before it began showing its age.

When you discover this classy gem, all polished and new again, you'll discover one of the traditions that road-weary travelers especially appreciate: a genuinely friendly and helpful staff. Enjoy afternoon tea in the grand Tea Court, looking just as it did in 1927, including its paneling of polished eucalyptus, or try a cold beverage, along with late-afternoon hors d'oeuvres, in the nearby marble and mirrored bar or in the intimate mezzanine lounge.

Then settle into leather armchairs in the hotel's elegantly casual restaurant. Here guests can sample the chef's award-winning Northwest cuisine—including freshly cooked entrées from the ocean, farms, and fields—during each of the four seasons. The guest rooms and suites are comfortable nests decorated in warm earth tones, accented with soft English chintzes covering rattan sofas, armchairs, and queen-size beds. Green plants add a fresh, outdoorsy touch. For additional information and reservations, contact the manager, Mary Arnstad, and her staff at the Heathman Hotel, SW Broadway at Salmon Street, Portland 97205 (503–241–4100).

Music and theater lovers can also check out summertime offerings, some outdoors, for the following: **Your Zoo and All That Jazz,** in July and August (503–226–1561); the fabulous **Mount Hood Festival of Jazz,** during the first weekend of August (503–666–3810); and Brown Bag concerts, at the Old Church downtown (503–222–2031). When you get to town, pick up a copy of *Willamette Week* and the *Downtowner* for current listings of stage, theater, gallery, and film offerings, as well as bistro and restaurant listings and reviews.

WHERE THE RIVERS MERGE

For another pleasant excursion head north and west of downtown via Twenty-third Avenue to access Highway 30, and then drive about 10 miles to **Sauvie Island,** a pastoral area lying along the confluence of the Willamette River from the south and the Columbia River from the east. The island was settled in the late 1840s, and at one time some forty dairy farms were scattered about it. The southern half now contains lush strawberry and raspberry fields, fruit orchards, and vegetable farms; many Sauvie Island farmers offer their homegrown fruit and produce in open-air stands all summer and into early autumn.

After crossing the Sauvie Island Bridge onto this flat, oblong island that is loved by weekend bicyclers, enjoy meandering along the quiet roads that nearly encircle the terrain. Take a detour to **Oak Island** for some serious bird-watching, canoe on tiny Sturgeon Lake or quiet Multnomah Channel, or bring your bicycle and pedal around the quiet byways. The northern half of the island—where Oak Island and Sturgeon Lake are located—remains a native wetlands area, the **Sauvie Island Wildlife Refuge.** Hundreds of birds migrating along the busy Pacific Flyway make pit stops here twice each year to rest and refuel.

Meriwether Lewis and William Clark also passed near this area on their trek to the Northwest during the early 1800s. On November 3, 1805, Clark, while camped along the Columbia River and feeling somewhat disgruntled, wrote in his journal that the party couldn't sleep "for the noise kept up during the whole of the night by the swans, Geese, white & Grey Brant, Ducks, & c on a small Sand Island. . . . They were imensely numerous, and their noise horid."

With the aid of binoculars, you'll probably spot Canada geese, snow geese, white-fronted geese, assorted ducks, and smaller birds and wildlife. Without binoculars, however, you'll probably still see many larger birds, such as marsh and red-tailed hawks, vultures, tundra swans, sandhill cranes, and blue herons. During winter a population of about thirty bald eagles roosts in an old-growth forest some miles away, leisurely commuting to Sauvie Island at sunrise to spend the day.

Because something like 500,000 acres of U.S. "wetlands"—a composite description for ponds, lakes, and sloughs and their adjacent grasslands and meadows loved by waterfowl, other birds, and wildlife—are being drained and filled each year, the numbers of birds using the Pacific Flyway has changed dramatically since the days of the Lewis and Clark expedition. For helpful information about efforts to conserve wetlands in the Portland area, including a schedule of bird-watching treks to Sauvie Island and other nearby wildlife habitats, contact James Davis, the education director, or Mike Houck, an urban naturalist, at the **Portland Audubon Society,** 5151 SW Cornell Road, Portland 97210 (503–292–6855). Better yet, stop by the society's visitors' center on your way from downtown Portland, via Lovejoy Street (head west), for maps and bird-watching lists before continuing out to Sauvie Island. The headquarters of the Sauvie Island Wildlife Refuge can be reached at (503) 621–3488.

James Bybee House & Agricultural Museum

While you're exploring the island, stop at the ◆ **James Bybee House and Agricultural Museum,** circa 1850, at Howell Territorial Park. In the pioneer orchard you can inspect 115 varieties of apple trees; in the restored farmhouse you can see vintage furnishings and, on the second floor, a wonderful children's room; and in the side yard you can have a picnic amid the collection of old, scented roses. Be sure, too, to poke into the huge barn to see pioneer farm equipment, sacks of grain, and old-time wagons. The pungent aroma of hay and grain may remind you of visiting your grandparents' farm in the country.

Reaching the farmstead is simple: After crossing the Multnomah Channel on the Sauvie Island Bridge from Highway 30, follow the signs to 13801 NW Howell Park Road and down the lane to the large parking area. The Bybee House is open June through Labor Day, Wednesday through Sunday, from noon to 5:00 P.M.; a schedule of annual events can be obtained from the Oregon Historical Society, 1230 SW Park Avenue, Portland 97205. The Wintering-In festival takes place on the last Saturday in September and offers freshly pressed cider, demonstrations of pioneer handicrafts, and a sale of old photographs as well as games for children, live music, and tours of the Bybee House.

You could also stay the night on the island by arranging quarters at **Sauvie Island Bed & Breakfast.** Perched on the bank of the Columbia River and with views of four of those ice-cream-cone mountain peaks in the Cascades, you can enjoy vegetables from island gardens plus a delicious country breakfast served by innkeepers Marie and A.J. Colasurdo. For information and reservations the address and telephone are 26504 NW Reeder Road, Portland 97231; (503) 621–3216. Incidentally, for a copy of the latest *Oregon Bed & Breakfast Directory,* a statewide listing of Oregon homes away from home, write to Bette Hammer, Coordinator, P.O. Box 1283, Grants Pass 97526, or call her at (800) 841–5448.

If time allows, continue west out Highway 30 about 12 miles farther, toward St. Helens, to enjoy a panoramic view from the historic waterfront area of this circa 1844 city. Find ◆**Columbia View Park** just next door to the courthouse; then post yourself at the old-fashioned gazebo or the brick viewing platform and watch the powerboats, sailboats, and barges on the river. One of the Beaver State's oldest cities, St. Helens is located at the confluence of the Columbia River and the Multnomah Channel on the Oregon side. The Lewis River and Bachelor Island Slough are to the north on the Washington side.

At **Bayport Marina** on Scappoose Bay, just south of Columbia View Park, you'll find boat-launch and picnic facilities. The

St. Helens Sailing Club holds weekly sailboat races here from April through August, and on the Fourth of July a stunning display of fireworks explodes over offshore Sand Island. For more information about annual events and historic inns in the area, contact the St. Helens Visitors' Information Center, 174 South Columbia Highway, St. Helens 97051 (503–397–0685).

HISTORIC EAST SIDE NEIGHBORHOODS

Enjoy visiting a bevy of secondhand stores and antiques shops in ◆**Historic Sellwood Neighborhood,** via Macadam Avenue and Sellwood Bridge, located just south of the downtown and old town areas. This old neighborhood, with its small homes and tidy lawns, skirts the Willamette River's east bank near the Sellwood Bridge and Oaks Park. Amble along SE Thirteenth Avenue, stopping for lunch or tea and dessert at one of the many delis or small restaurants in the area, or take a picnic down to the new park along the river, just north of the bridge, or to Westmoreland Park, where you can watch youngsters and oldsters sail their boats on the large pond. You'll find comfortable benches for sitting and enjoying the view all along the west side of the pond. Access Westmoreland Park just off Bybee Boulevard near Twentieth Avenue.

Then went your way over to the ◆**Hawthorne Neighborhood,** just north of the Sellwood area, via Seventeenth or Thirty-ninth avenues. On Hawthorne Boulevard, between Fortieth and Twentieth avenues, you'll find a restored area of interesting shops, delis, restaurants, and boutiques. Stop by Dragonfly Gardens, near Twenty-second, for a good selection of plants and garden-related goodies; snoop through the Hawthorne Coffee Merchant, near Thirty-fifth Avenue, for gourmet coffees, teas, and candies; have lunch at Pastaworks, near Thirty-seventh, or at Bread and Ink Cafe, near Thirty-sixth Avenue. For a real treat stop in at ◆**Grand Central Bakery** for outstanding cinnamon rolls, scones, and espresso as well as the rustic Italian breads for which the bakery has become famous: thick, crested, free form, and very chewy, made by slow-rise and long-fermentation processes. Among the greatest hits are the Como loaf, rustic baguette, Sole Mio, sour white round, and rosemary roll. Find the bakery at 2230 SE Hawthorne Boulevard. The telephone number is (503) 232–0575.

Then, too, if you love exceptional bagels, stop by **Big Bear Bagel Bakery & Cafe,** located nearby at 1852 SE Hawthorne Boulevard. Large and chewy, the bagels are rated among the city's best and are freshly baked every day. The cafe, which offers tasty soups, fresh salads, and piping-hot espresso, is open weekdays from 7:00 A.M. to 3:00 P.M. and Friday through Sunday from 7:00 A.M. to 7:00 P.M. The telephone number is (503) 238–7647.

Continue east on Hawthorne Boulevard toward 600-foot **Mt. Tabor** for a view of the city from atop one of Portland's extinct volcanic cinder cones. For the best view wind up to the top, where you'll be sheltered beneath towering Douglas fir, their long branches swaying in the gentle breezes like graceful ballerinas. Below are the city's water reservoirs, which hold water from the Bull Run watershed area located in the Cascade foothills east of Sandy and Highway 26. Picnic tables are located in shaded or sunny spots here and there, and you can hike around the park for views of snowcapped Mt. Hood, also to the east.

You can also discover comfortable places to spend the night on the east side of town. One of the coziest, a 1908 Dutch Colonial faced with clinker bricks, is tucked into a side street just north of the **Lloyd Center** shops and ice arena. Here Peggie and Bob Irvine welcome travelers to the **Clinkerbrick House Bed and Breakfast,** where, amid Peggie's collections—including antiques, quilts, and strawberries—guests find a comfortable home away from home. Three spacious suites on the second floor offer quiet havens after a busy day of seeing the city; an example is the lovely Garden Room, with its wicker chaise longue and canopied queen-size bed, a cozy room that gets the morning sun. You can also use the common room on the second floor, which has books and magazines, a color television, a microwave oven, and a small refrigerator stocked with complimentary soft drinks.

Peggie's gourmet breakfasts are the kind you'll write home about—you might be served Eggs Bravato with salsa, sour cream, and avocado; Ricotta Pancakes with fresh blueberries and warm blueberry syrup; and fresh seasonal fruits, Apricot Breakfast Roll, Oregon Plum Cobbler Cake, and cinnamon rolls. For further information and reservations, contact the Irvines at 2311 NE Schuyler Street, Portland 97212 (503–281–2533). Children are welcome as well.

Should the Clinkerbrick House be booked up when you call, ask about **Georgian House** and **Portland's White House,** two other fine bed-and-breakfast inns located in this area. Also nearby are the Memorial Coliseum and new Convention Center, where numerous sports and other public events are held throughout the year.

If the kids are along, plan a stop at the ◆**Carousel Courtyard,** located at the west end of the Lloyd Center and in the Holladay Market area, near NE Seventh and Ninth streets at Holladay Street. The courtyard, which is wheelchair-accessible, features an 1895 Looff carousel, a children's theater workshop, and the **International Carousel Museum.** The carousel operates Monday through Saturday from 11:00 A.M. to 5:00 P.M. and Sunday from noon to 5:00 P.M.

On the east side of town, a pleasant place to eat lunch is ◆**Albertina's Restaurant.** You can also browse for cards, jewelry, and gift items in the **Kerr Gift Shop** and for antiques, collectibles, and secondhand items in **Kerr's Economy Jar.** All these are located in the Old Kerr Nursery at 424 NE Twenty-second Avenue. The Georgian Revival building was home to more than 200 homeless children from 1921 to 1967. Today the agency, named for the young wife of Alexander Kerr, an early Portland resident and developer and manufacturer of the Kerr jar lid, provides services in foster care, maternity and adoption, care of the multiple handicapped, and family counseling and operates a residential youth center. The restaurant is open for lunch Monday through Friday and reservations are recommended for either of the two seatings, at 11:30 A.M. or 1:00 P.M. For further information call the volunteer staff at (503) 231–0216.

OREGON TRAIL'S END

Those blue-sky afternoons often beckon young and old alike to the **Willamette River,** just as they did when those first pioneers arrived and settled near the base of the falls at Oregon City. In the late 1800s the Willamette River was the "main street" for life in the Willamette Valley: People traveled by riverboats and stern-wheelers, produce and supplies were shipped in and out by steamboats, and Oregon's principal cities started as river towns and steamboat landings. No fewer than seven major cities are located along the river, and more than half the people in Oregon live within 10 miles of the

Willamette; in fact more than sixty percent of all Oregonians live within the Willamette River Basin.

One of the best ways to cool off and see this historic area from a different perspective is to take a boat ride upriver about 18 miles, south toward Lake Oswego, West Linn, Milwaukie, Gladstone, and Oregon City. The boat proceeds south from downtown Portland, first maneuvering under the Ross Island Bridge, and then continues upriver past tiny Ross Island toward the Sellwood area. Sunlight sparkles from the moving water, and the city skyline recedes in midafternoon's golden light. The air smells fresh and clean.

Cruising upriver at a comfortable speed, the boat may pass a flotilla of small sailboats engaged in a race. White sails catch the wind, and sunlight turns them brightly translucent. Tinkly music from the **Oaks Park** merry-go-round wafts across the water as the boat passes under the Sellwood Bridge, continuing south toward the small communities along both banks of the river and the historic Willamette Falls at Oregon City.

A profusion of greenery passes by—cool canopies of trees, shrubbery, and mosses clinging to basaltic ledges and rocky walls here and there on both east and west banks of the river. The boat cruises past waterside homes; a small pontoon plane crouches at its dockside resting place; water-skiers glide past on wide skis; and great blue herons—Portland's official bird—and seagulls catch the wind overhead.

At **Clackamette Park,** near Gladstone and Oregon City, peer over the railing to see where the smaller Clackamas River quietly enters the Willamette. The boat passes beneath the Interstate 205 and old Oregon City bridges, toward the falls.

Nearing the falls, the boat maneuvers away from them and around to the entrance to the ◆**Willamette Falls Locks,** the early settlers' solution to the water problem of navigating the river at this point. Someone jumps onto the dock and yanks the rope, which, in turn, activates a light and horn alerting the lock tender. If there's no tugboat coming through the locks from upriver, your boat will be next in line.

The giant wooden doors soon open wide, and the boat moves into the first of the four watery chambers. The lock master waves from the small station, keeping track of the gates and traffic on a television monitor while relaying instructions to the second lock tender in the upper station. It takes about thirty minutes to reach the upper Willamette River channel above the falls with the help of the historic locks. Constructed in 1872 by Chinese laborers, the locks have operated since 1873. In 1974 the project was placed on the National Register of Historic Places, and in 1991 the American Society of Civil Engineers, Oregon Section, designated the locks a national civil engineering landmark. *Note:* Midweek, after 5:00 P.M., is the best time to enter the locks without waiting; such delays can run thirty or forty minutes on a busy summer weekend.

Its passengers warmed by the late-afternoon sun, the boat then cruises upriver a couple of miles before returning through the locks to the lower channel and heading downriver, past Clackamette Park and waterside homes. A great blue heron balances long, spindly legs on a rock outcropping, and the city reappears, a surreal image of thick vertical lines on the sunset horizon.

Stern-wheelers resurrected from yesteryear are once again cruising up both the Willamette and the Columbia rivers. To join one of the cruises on either river, check with the stern-wheeler *Columbia Gorge,* which makes frequent trips. The office is located at 1200 NW Front Street, Suite 110, in Portland; the telephone number is (503) 223–3928. For smaller charter boats inquire at the visitors' center in downtown Portland, (503) 222–2223.

If you would like to visit the Willamette Falls Locks and arranging a boat ride isn't feasible, you can drive from Portland south via Macadam Avenue and Highway 43 through Lake Oswego to West Linn. Drive under the Interstate 205 bridge, continue to the red brick building housing West Linn City Hall, and look for the sign—just before crossing the old Oregon City bridge—that says WILLAMETTE FALLS LOCKS AND ARMY CORPS OF ENGINEERS. Don't give up—it's well worth the effort to find this out-of-the-way gem. Park nearby and follow the paved walk and series of concrete stairs that lead down to the public viewing area.

Just for fun, spend a couple of hours on land watching tugboats, barges, pleasure boats, and perhaps a party of canoes pass through the four lock chambers. The lock tenders are a congenial lot and are usually pleased to answer questions about the historic locks; there is a large grassy area with shade trees, picnic tables, and sunny spots. The public rest rooms are wheelchair-accessible. The small Historical Museum on the grounds, offering detailed information and wide-angle photographs of the construction of the four lock chambers, is open daily from 8:00 A.M. to 5:00 P.M. For additional information contact the Lockmaster, John Wasson, Willamette Falls Locks, U.S. Army Corps of Engineers, West Linn 97068. The telephone number is (503) 656–3381.

While in the area, drive up behind the West Linn High School, just above the city hall building, to find one of the region's smallest preserves, **Camassia Natural Area.** In a tangled, natural woodland of Oregon white oak, madrone, and Douglas fir, the preserve's delicate wildflower meadows and rocky areas, stands of maple and cottonwood, and willow swales and ponds allow a close-up look at an array of native plant life. In mid- to late April, the grassy plateaus bloom with purple camas and large-flowered collinsia, while in the shaded areas delicate fawn lilies, trilliums, and western wild ginger bloom. The only discordant note in this idyllic spot is an abundance of poison oak. (*Note:* Most everyone is allergic to every part of the plant.) For information about all thirty-two preserves on some 35,000 acres throughout the state, contact the Oregon field office of the **Nature Conservancy,** 1234 NW Twenty-fifth Avenue, Portland 97210. Conservancy naturalists ask that visitors stay on the trails to protect the delicate habitat here; don't pick the fragile wildflowers, and don't bring dogs into the preserve. Access the parking area from Walnut Street.

To visit the tiny community of Willamette, the most historic part of West Linn, head west on the frontage road, Willamette Falls Drive, above the locks and the Willamette River for a couple of miles. Here you'll find a couple of antiques shops, several eateries, a large city park along the river (great spot for a picnic), and, a bit farther, just off Dollar Street, the **Oregon Grape Nursery and Footpath Cafe.** After browsing among the luscious hanging fuchsia and flowering begonia baskets, snoop through the well-stocked gift shop and enjoy an espresso or a latte on the outside deck if the weather permits. This charming place is open Monday through Saturday from 8:00 A.M. to 6:00 P.M. and on Sundays from 9:30 A.M. to 6:00 P.M.

Just east, after you've crossed the Willamette River from West Linn via the old **Highway 99 Oregon City Bridge,** you'll find historic Oregon City, which boasts the distinction of being the first incorporated city west of the Rocky Mountains. In the winter of 1829–30, however, there were just three log houses here, and in the following spring, the first vegetables—potatoes—were planted. Apparently the local Native Americans resented this infringement on their territory and burned the houses. A flour mill and a sawmill, constructed near the falls in 1832 by the British Hudson's Bay Company, made use of the first waterpower in the territory.

The immigration over the Oregon Trail in 1844 added several hundred folks to Oregon City's population. The provisional government body, formed in 1843 at Champoeg, located on the banks of the Willamette River south and west a few miles, chose Oregon City as its seat; the first provisional legislature assembled here in June 1844, at the Rose Farm.

By 1846 Oregon City contained some seventy houses and about 500 citizens. In January 1848 Joe Meek carried the request of the provisional legislature for territorial status to President James K. Polk in Washington, D.C. Meek returned in March 1849 with the newly appointed territorial governor, Joseph Lane. Oregon City was made the territorial capital and remained so until 1852, when the seat of government was moved to Salem, some 50 miles south, in the heart of the Willamette Valley.

To begin your tour stop first at the **End of the Oregon Trail Interpretive Center,** located at Fifth and Washington. The center houses paintings and memorabilia illustrating and explaining the rigorous, 2,000-mile journey from Independence, Missouri, to Oregon City—both the land route to The Dalles, including the float on crudely made barges down the swift and dangerous Columbia River, and the alternate Barlow Trail route, forged over Mt. Hood. Of the 300,000 immigrants who undertook this formidable trek, some 30,000 died on the way and were buried along the trail. The interpretive center is open Tuesday through Saturday from 10:00 A.M. to 4:00 P.M. and Sunday from noon to 4:00 P.M. Call (503) 657–9336 for more information.

The 150th anniversary of the Oregon Trail migration was celebrated in 1993. For a complete list of events planned for other historic celebrations and local festivals, write to the Oregon City Visitors' Information Center at 1795 Washington Street, Oregon City 97045 (503–656–1619) or to the Clackamas County Historical Society, 211 Tumwater Street (P.O. Box 294), Oregon City 97045 (503–655–5574).

Next, pick up the *Historic Walking Tour* brochure and map, park on Main Street near the courthouse, and walk a few blocks to the **Oregon City Municipal Elevator,** accessing it via the lower entrance, on Railroad Avenue at Seventh Street. You'll enjoy the thirty-second vertical ride up the face of the 90-foot basalt cliff—the city is built on two levels. The elevator—one of only four municipal elevators in the world—replaced the old Indian trails and pioneer paths that originally led from river's edge to the top of the basalt bluff.

The first elevator, which took three minutes to travel up and down, was powered by water. It was constructed in 1915—much to the chagrin of citizen Sara Chase, who objected to its location in front of her Victorian mansion. Not only did Sara never use the municipal elevator, but she had a heavy wrought-iron fence erected so that "none of those elevator people" could trespass on her property. On the interior wall of the observation area atop the elevator, you can see an artist's painting of the Chase mansion.

Walk south a few blocks along the upper **Promenade** (it's also wheelchair-accessible) for a spectacular view of the falls. Imagine what the area must have been like before the settlers arrived, before power lines and buildings, before bridges and freeways and automobiles. Actually the first long-distance transmission of electricity in the United States happened here—from Oregon City to Portland, in 1888.

The early Native American families fished for salmon along the forested riverbanks amid stands of Douglas fir, the blue sky overhead and the roar of the falls ever present. The falls cascade some 42 feet over several basaltic ledges in the middle of the wide river. You can sit at any of the public benches along the Promenade, basking in the late-afternoon sun while imagining a bit of Oregon history.

Continuing a few blocks north and east, visit the historic ◆**McLoughlin House,** which was the home of Dr. John McLoughlin, a dominant figure in not only the Hudson's Bay Company but also the early development of the region. Appointed chief factor, or superintendent of trade, of the British company in 1824, the tall, white-haired, cane-carrying man ruled over the entire Columbia country before the Oregon Trail migration began in 1843.

Under orders from the Hudson's Bay Company, McLoughlin established the first settlement at Oregon City and moved here from **Fort Vancouver,** across the Columbia River, when he resigned from the company in 1845. Incidentally, reconstructed

McLoughlin House

Fort Vancouver and its newly reclaimed British-style vegetable, herb, and flower gardens are well worth a visit. The stockade, including living history in the kitchen quarters, baking quarters, general store, blacksmith shop, and main house, all provided by National Park Service staff and volunteers, is located just across the Columbia River from Portland, near downtown Vancouver, Washington. Further information and directions can be obtained from the McLoughlin House staff. Born in the Canadian province of Quebec, Dr. McLoughlin became a U.S. citizen in 1851 and spent his later years operating his store, gristmill, and sawmills near the base of the Willamette Falls.

McLoughlin's mansion, a large clapboard-style building with simple, dignified lines, was saved from the wrecker's ball and moved from its original location along the Willamette River near the falls up to the top of the bluff and placed in McLoughlin Park at Seventh and Center streets. On the lovely grounds are large rhododendrons, clumps of azaleas, and old roses, and to the rear of the house sits a moss-covered fountain, shaded by tall Douglas firs and trailing ivy. For information about the annual Candlelight Holiday Tour and the August Family Festival, contact the curator of the McLoughlin House, Nancy Wilson, at 713 Center Street, Oregon City 97045 (503–656–5146). The house is open Tuesday through Saturday from 10:00 A.M. to 4:00 P.M. and Sunday from 1:00 to 4:00 P.M., except on holidays and during the month of January.

For a tasty treat, stop at the **Fellows House Restaurant and Inn** for lunch in a restored, circa 1867 Gothic Revival structure, painted a cheerful peach with white trim and surrounded by a lovely flower garden. It's located on McLoughlin Boulevard—old Highway 99E—in the **Canemah Historic District,** just beyond the **Clackamas County Historical Society Center,** both just south of the Oregon City Municipal Elevator. Refurbished by Tom and Mary DeHaven in the spring of 1989, the Fellows House also has three comfortable bed-and-breakfast guest rooms on its second floor. The second-level balcony, across the front of the inn, offers splendid views of the Willamette River and falls. Captain Fellows, who built the house, was a shipbuilder, a ship engineer, and a stern-wheeler captain on the river during those early years when it served as the region's "main street."

Guests are served the Captain's Special Breakfast in one of the two dining areas on the main level; the fare includes freshly squeezed juices, special egg and bacon dishes, and steaming-hot gourmet coffee and teas. For lunch, with tables open to the public, Tom creates specialty sandwiches like the Canemah, with Dungeness crabmeat, melted cheddar, avocado, onion, tomato, lettuce, and the inn's special sauce, all on Sourdough Willy's fresh-baked bread. (You can stop at Sourdough Willy's, by the way, for deli breads and brownies when you drive from Lake Oswego to West Linn; it's on the right, just beyond Marylhurst College.)

For information and reservations contact the DeHavens at the Fellows House, 416 South McLoughlin Boulevard, Oregon City 97045 (503–656–2089). The inn's restaurant is open Monday through Friday from 11:00 A.M. to 3:00 P.M.

You can also stay overnight in a circa 1880 vernacular-style house in Oregon City's Historic District—the **Jagger House Bed and Breakfast,** restored by Claire and Tom Met, who live right next door in another vintage home that reportedly has its very own resident ghost. Louis Jagger, after whom the inn is named, was a local greengrocer who accompanied his parents across the Oregon Trail to Oregon City in the late 1860s; by then the trail was a well-worn road of sorts.

The Jagger House is within walking distance of several museums, including the Stevens Crawford House Museum, the McLoughlin House, and the End of the Oregon Trail Interpretive Center. Claire and Tom also have a couple of bicycles you can borrow to pedal around the upper section of town, exploring to your heart's content. Pick up a deli picnic at **Simply Devine Deli,** just around the corner at Seventh and Washington streets, and enjoy eating at the inn's picnic table, set in a latticed arbor in the private side garden. The Garden Delight guest room has its own entrance just off the garden level and offers a comfortable haven of white wicker furnishings; a painted antique, queen-size bed; and deep burgundy carpeting.

On the second floor are two other guest rooms, Victorian Rose and Country Charm. Enjoy the main-level common area for reading, conversation, or working on the resident jigsaw puzzle. In the dining room Claire serves a delicious breakfast, which may include cinnamon French toast, banana pancakes, cheese and sausage strata, a veggie or shrimp frittata, or a German pancake with sautéed cinnamon apples. For information and reservations contact the Mets at the Jagger House, 512 Sixth Street in Oregon City 97045 (503–657–7820). Claire is also an active member of the Old Home Forum and can help guests with a historic walking tour of the area.

Another rural loop from Oregon City offers a ramble into the eastern section of Clackamas County, reaching into the foothills of the Cascade Mountains. Take the Park Place exit from Interstate 205 and turn left at the first light, toward Park Place. Settle into the slow lane and wind along Clackamas River Drive toward Carver. Rather than crossing the river here just yet, continue east on Springwater Road; then just beyond the boat-ramp entrance, turn right for about a quarter-mile to the **German Methodist Church** and the **Baker Cabin.**

The small church, built around 1895, sits like a tidy little dowager under tall firs surrounded by well-kept grounds. Walk the gravel drive to the far end of the grassy area to inspect the Baker Cabin, which dates to 1856; notice the old grapevine, with its enormous main trunk, which must have been planted around the same time as the cabin was built. The logs were hand-hewn into square-shaped timbers that deftly interlock at the four corners. Tiny ferns and wildflowers grow from crevices in the old rock fireplace chimney at the west end of the cabin. For information about the annual Pioneer Bazaar and other events open to the public, contact the Baker Cabin Historical Society, P.O. Box 741, Oregon City 97045 (503–631–8274). The cabin and church are located at the corner of Hattan and Gronlund roads.

Now backtrack to the Carver bridge, cross the Clackamas River and angle to your left onto Highway 224 to feast your eyes on one woman's spectacular flower garden, ◆ **Tallina's Garden,** located at 15790 SE Highway 224. Usually the first thing visitors notice is the large lath dome and extensive pergola atop a small knoll just south of the main house. Built to replicate a similar one seen in a French garden, this forms an impressive backdrop for Tallina George's lavish rose garden, growing in terraced beds just below. The intimate knot-garden design was copied from the Barnsley House garden of Gloucestershire, England. You'll also find several intimate "garden rooms" filled with luscious roses, annuals, perennials, and vegetables, too. A gazebo is covered with roses as well. At last count this lover of gardens had planted more than a thousand rose varieties that now climb up posts, sprawl over walls, and line walkways. Although it is a private garden, Tallina George welcomes visitors to park in the large parking area and stroll through her beautiful creation. She asks that children be supervised by adults. You may also enjoy visiting the large white barn that houses her fabric-and-lace business.

From Tallina's you can head farther off the beaten path by taking Highway 224 back toward the Clackamas River but heading, this time, east and south about 15 miles to Estacada to find **Harmony Bakery,** tucked away at SW Second and Wade streets. Here you can join a diverse group of local folks who meet to drink coffee, eat Linda Lawrence's freshly made bagels, and, of course, have a good-morning or afternoon chat about the weather and the state of the world's economic affairs. A bagel with cream cheese to go is still just 50 cents, or you could order the omelet with spicy hash-brown potatoes, vegetarian fare, or more traditional sandwiches and burgers. The restaurant is open Monday through Saturday from 7:00 A.M. to 3:00 P.M. and on Sundays from 8:00 A.M. to 3:00 P.M.

From Estacada continue south another 15 miles or so via Highway 211 to Molalla to discover **Pacific Northwest Live Steamers,** a miniature railroad park set in the Cascade foothills of eastern Clackamas County. Congenial volunteer engineers, members of the Pacific Northwest Live Steamers Club, run miniature trains on some 6,000 feet of track from noon to 5:00 P.M. on Sundays, May through October. There's a shady picnic area nearby in the park.

Riding with the kids in one of the small open-air cars behind your "Sunday engineer" is reminiscent of one's childhood days, dreaming of choo-choo trains, clanging bells, and whistle blasts. Two long toots signal "start" or "release brakes"; a long and a short mean "warning"; three shorts when a train is stopped designate "back up"; and one long whistle indicates the train is approaching a station. The miniature engine huffs and puffs steam from a tiny smokestack, just like its full-size original counterpart: the sleek steam locomotive that replaced horse-drawn wagons as well as the Pony Express and helped to settle the west.

In recent decades these mechanical marvels have all but disappeared, especially the steam locomotives, although many full-size models are also being restored and put back into service for nostalgic weekend trips; examples are the **Mt. Hood Railroad** in Hood River, the **Sumpter Valley Railroad** in Sumpter, near Baker City, and the **Oregon Coastline Express** in Tillamook. Pacific Northwest Live Steamers miniature railroad park is located at 31083 S. Shady Dell Drive in Molalla; call (503) 829–6866 for more information. To access the park from Highway 211, drive into Molalla and turn south at the Y-Grocery for about ½ mile, then west onto Feyrer Park Road to Shady Dell Park.

FARM AND FLOWER COUNTRY

From Molalla complete your rural loop by heading west on Highway 211 to Woodburn and turning north on old Highway 99E through Hubbard to Aurora, Canby, and back to Oregon City. Old Highway 99, which divides into two sections, 99E and 99W, as it winds through Willamette Valley towns, was the first paved north-south route (it followed sections of the early stagecoach route) linking all cities and towns along the Willamette River and south into the Umpqua and Rogue river valleys. From my childhood in the 1940s, I remember trips on old Highway 99 that took seven "long" hours of driving from Grants Pass, in southern Oregon, to Portland.

Although one can now whiz up and down sleek Interstate 5, covering the same distance in about four and a half hours, once in a while it's nice to get off the freeway and ramble along sections of old Highway 99 and its rural tributaries. It's a nostalgic trek into yesterday for native Oregonians, one generously shared with visitors.

Pull off Highway 99E in Aurora to visit the ◆ **Aurora National Historic District** and the Old Aurora Colony Museum, which inhabits a large, refurbished ox barn. The colony's history began in the Harmony Colony in Pennsylvania, from which William Keil, a German tailor, physician, and preacher, and his followers emigrated to found the town of Bethel, Missouri, near the start of the Oregon Trail.

Most of the members of Keil's colony were mechanics, working on wagons for those who were preparing to head west on the Oregon Trail from Independence, Missouri. In 1855 Keil led a group to Oregon to begin a second colony, one he named Aurora, after his daughter. All businesses and properties were owned by the community, rather than by individuals, and the peaceful farm colony thrived until Keil's death in 1877. Although the commune then disbanded and divided the land and other group-owned assets, many families remained and still live in the Aurora-Hubbard area.

Some of the historic landmarks have vanished over the years, but many of the buildings remain, including the ox barn that houses the museum, a small log cabin, a washhouse, a machine shed, an assortment of farm machinery, and a lovely garden, the **Emma Wakefield Herb Garden.** The colony was well known for its fine cooking and music; its brass band entertained at community festivities and events. In the museum you'll see many of the brass instruments, including the *schellenbaum,* a rare bell tree.

The museum has an excellent collection of historic quilts made by various women of the commune, and many of these quilts are displayed throughout the year. In February the **Zion Mennonite Quilters,** in nearby Hubbard, along with the Aurora Colony Historical Society, offer hands-on quilting workshops, handcrafted items, and refreshments. Quilters have met for more than seventy years at the Zion Mennonite Church. Further information about other annual events, such as the Spinner's Festival, can be obtained from the Old Aurora Colony Museum, Second and Liberty streets, Aurora 97002

(503–678–5754). The museum complex is open Wednesday through Saturday from 10:00 A.M. to 4:30 P.M., with the addition of Tuesday from June through August, and is closed during January.

As you head toward Canby from Aurora, you can take another side ramble by turning east onto Barlow Road and proceeding about 4 miles to **St. Josef's Winery.** Owners Lilli and Josef Fleischmann decided to trade the bakery business for wine making about ten years ago. In 1983, their first year as vintners, St. Josef's Cabernet won the Consumer's Choice award at a festival in Spokane, Washington.

Join the congenial crowd at the annual **Grape Stomping Festival,** held the first weekend of October, or take a picnic along during the spring and summer months and sit under enormous redwood trees at one of the tables on the grounds. In the tasting room you can sample Oregon Rieslings, gewürztraminers, and several varieties of zinfandel, as well as the most recent Pinot noirs. Located at 28836 S. Barlow Road, St. Josef's Winery is open daily from noon to 5:00 P.M., and the tables usually remain outdoors until cool weather begins, around the end of October. Call (503) 651–3190 for more information.

As you head back toward Canby on Barlow Road to Highway 99E, notice the large fields of tulips and other bulbs that bloom during mid-April. In these far southern reaches of Clackamas County, the rich alluvial soils from ancient rivers support more than a hundred nurseries, where growers raise everything from annuals and perennials to ornamentals and fruit stock. You can also see, just west of Aurora, acres and acres of lush green turf grass, which is cut into strips and rolled into compact bundles destined for someone's new lawn.

Most of the nurseries are the wholesale variety, shipping to destinations throughout the United States, but a few are open to the public. Near Canby, just a few miles west of the downtown area, visit **Swan Island Dahlias** and wander through some forty acres of the gorgeous perennials that bloom in late summer, beginning in August and lasting until the first frost, sometime in mid- to late October.

This large nursery has been operated by the Gitts family since the 1950s, and dahlias have been part of the Canby area since the late 1940s. The farm features more than 250 varieties, with blooms ranging from 12 or more inches in diameter to those of tiny pompons, at less than 2 inches across. The voluptuous flowers are reported to have originated in Mexico and were brought back from the New World by the explorer Cortés. Since that time, the newer hybrids have been developed for stronger stems, to better support the large heavy flowers. Walk through the labeled rows to find selections like Gay Princess, Cuddles, Sassy, Cameo, Matchmaker, and First Love—visitors can even select and purchase a take-along bouquet.

From Canby access Swan Island Dahlias from Ivy Street to Second Street, then Holly Street to Twenty-second Street. During the farm's indoor Dahlia Show, usually held the second weekend of September, you can watch professional designers fashion the vibrant blooms into creative arrangements. If you miss that event, you can still stroll through the blooming fields, beginning in August, Monday through Friday from 9:00 A.M. to 4:30 P.M. Call (503) 266–7711 for further information.

To delve into more history about the area, stop at the **Canby Depot Museum** at the north edge of town. The museum, maintained by the Canby Area Historical Society, is housed in the oldest railroad station owned by the C & C Railroad. The restored building is just off Highway 99E at the Fairgrounds exit and is open weekdays from 10:00 A.M. to 4:00 P.M. and Saturday and Sunday from 1:00 to 4:00 P.M. Call (503) 266–9421 for more information. To inquire about the old-fashioned **Clackamas County Fair,** one of the best late-summertime events in the area, contact the Canby Visitors' Information Center, at 237 NW Second Street 97013 (503–266–4600).

If you're in the area around the second weekend of August, plan to join the happy throng attending the annual **Tualatin Crawfish Festival,** held in Tualatin City Park, just west of Interstate 5. A ton of cooked, spiced crawfish arrives via refrigerated truck on Saturday morning, and some 10,000 folks munch their way through 2,000 pounds of succulent crustaceans—now, that's an impressive bit of crawfish chomping. Members of the Sherwood Volunteer Fire Department usually serve barbecued chicken, just in case anyone wants to dine on something other than spiced "crawdads," and members of the Tualatin Historical Society offer fresh-baked breads, homemade jams, preserves, and lemonade as well.

Further information can be obtained from the Tualatin Visitors' Information Center, 18622 SW Boones Ferry Road, Tualatin 97062 (503–692–0780).

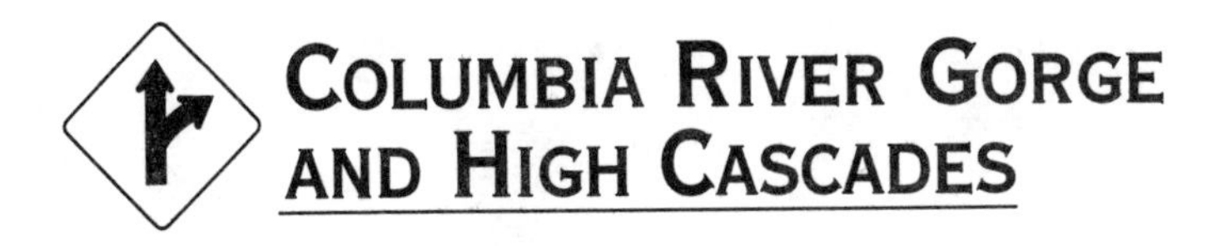

Columbia River Gorge and High Cascades

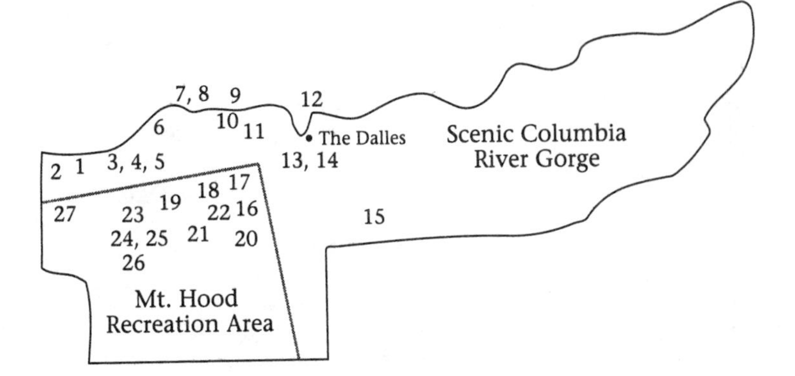

1. Columbia River Scenic Highway
2. Black Rabbit Restaurant and McMenamin's Edgefield
3. Multnomah Falls
4. Elowah Falls–McCord Creek
5. Gorge Hiking Weekend
6. Bonneville Dam
7. Port of Cascade Locks Marine Park
8. Bridge of the Gods
9. Hood River Boat Basin and Marina Park
10. Mt. Hood Railroad
11. Hood River Hotel
12. The Dalles Boat Basin Beach
13. Sorosis Park
14. Williams House Bed and Breakfast Inn
15. Balch Hotel
16. Mt. Hood
17. Sappington Orchards
18. Cooper Spur Inn and Ski Area
19. Barlow Road
20. Summit Meadows and Trillium Lake
21. Falcon's Crest Inn
22. Timberline Lodge
23. Salmon River National Recreation Trail
24. Heart of the Mountain Gifts and Treasures
25. Don Guidos Restaurant
26. Old Welches Bed and Breakfast Inn
27. Meining Memorial Park

Columbia River Gorge and High Cascades

Scenic Columbia River Gorge

Although much of the original winding highway, clinging alongside the Columbia River Gorge since 1915, has deteriorated or become part of streamlined Interstate 84, visitors can enjoy two good-size segments of the historic **Columbia River Scenic Highway** east of Portland between Troutdale and The Dalles.

Before heading east into the Columbia Gorge, particularly if you've not eaten, consider stopping in Troutdale to find the **Black Rabbit Restaurant** in the main lodge, a handsome Georgian Revival structure, at **McMenamins Edgefield.** It is located at 2126 SW Halsey Street, just south of Interstate 84 at the Wood Village exit. For dinner you might order such Northwest fare as salmon with hazelnut butter or clams steamed in ale. If time allows, you'll enjoy touring the twenty-five-acre complex that, in the early 1900s, housed the fully self-contained Multnomah County Poor Farm. Now completely restored, including an herb garden and small vineyard, the complex includes bed-and-breakfast lodging, meeting rooms, a winery and wine-cellar pub, an outdoor barbecue and picnic area, and, in the old power station, a brew pub and theater for showing vintage movies. The Black Rabbit Restaurant offers breakfast, lunch, and dinner daily. The telephone number is (503) 669–8610.

Punctuated with a dozen or more cascading waterfalls and enough hiking trails to keep outdoor buffs busy for weeks, the seventy-nine-year-old Scenic Highway offers a low-stress, relaxed alternative to busy Interstate 84. To access the first section of the old highway, detour from the freeway at the Lewis and Clark State Park exit east of McMenamin's Edgefield and Troutdale, just across the Sandy River.

The Scenic Highway parallels the east bank of the Sandy River and loops several miles through a sun-filtered canopy of big-leaf maples and Douglas fir, climbing gradually to the small community of Corbett. Just east of Corbett, pull into the **Women's Forum Park,** at **Chanticleer Point,** for one of the best panoramas of the Columbia River Gorge and the wide Columbia River, which separates Oregon and Washington.

The view is almost too vast to absorb. You'll see the massive stone **Vista House** perched atop **Crown Point** just a couple of miles distant; the silver ribbon of river shimmering some 750 feet below; then 800-foot **Beacon Rock,** a volcanic monolith about 25 miles upstream on the Washington side of the river; and the Union Pacific railroad tracks and Interstate 84, narrow ribbons paralleling the mighty river.

Samuel Hill, a Washingtonian and a lover of roads, inspired the building of the Scenic Highway. Combining forces with Samuel Lancaster, the consulting engineer, and Portland businessmen Simon Benson and John Yeon, Hill not only envisioned the economic and tourist potential of such a road but appreciated the aesthetic and natural beauty of the gorge as well. The highway's rapid completion date was prodded by Portland's desire to lure the state's turn-of-the-century motorists as well as travelers en route to the 1915 Panama Pacific Exhibition in California.

In the design of this first major highway in the Northwest, Lancaster incorporated graceful stone bridges, viaducts, stone walls, tunnels, and stone benches. He had been inspired by a trip to Europe with Sam Hill for the purpose of studying the historic Roman roads there. Alongside the Columbia River the ancient trail of deer, native peoples, and those first fur trappers was replaced with the functional yet beautiful highway that clung so closely to the gorge's lush moss, fern-covered, and tree-laden outcroppings. It is said that more than one early historian referred to the Scenic Highway as one of "poetry and drama."

Stop at the **Crown Point Visitors' Center** at Vista House for more camera clicking and history recollecting before winding down past Lancaster's graceful rock walls and roadside benches to **Latourell Falls.** Passing Shepperd's Dell, continue on to **Wahkeena Falls** (*Wahkeena* is an Indian word for "most beautiful"), where you'll find more parking and a large picnic area. Wahkeena tumbles and cascades in a series of frothy falls; dainty wildflowers bloom around rocks and in mossy crevices.

◆**Multnomah Falls,** just east of Latourell and Wahkeena Falls, is the most spectacular in the Columbia River Gorge, cascading in a long drop of 620 feet from the basaltic gorge rim. It's one of the highest waterfalls in the United States. If time allows, walk the easy trail to the upper bridge for a close encounter with the cascading water, accompanied by its swishing roar and cool mist.

An easy, though somewhat steep, trail continues from the bridge up to the rim for a top-of-the-falls, panoramic view of the world below. It's well worth the 2.4-mile round-trip trek, especially midweek, when you'll encounter fewer tourists. Take along some water or another beverage, and keep an eye out for poison oak, which lurks here and there along the trail's edge; the leaves look like a miniature oak leaf, and again, almost everyone is allergic to every part of the plant.

At the base of the falls, linger to visit rustic **Multnomah Falls Lodge,** also constructed in 1914–15, where breakfast, lunch, and dinner are served in a lovely atrium dining room; there are also a snack bar and a gift shop. Call (503) 695–2376 for dinner reservations.

East of Multnomah Falls, and still on the historic Scenic Highway section, is **Oneonta Gorge.** Oneonta Creek bubbles through the narrowest of high, mossy chasms here, and those who don't mind getting their feet wet can walk up the shallow creek to the cascading falls. Just east, however, a trail at **Horsetail Falls** leads behind the upper falls, crossing Oneonta Creek just before the water plunges over the rim in a frothy ribbon.

For helpful trail maps and hiking information, contact the Columbia River Gorge Ranger Station, 31520 SE Woodard Road, Troutdale 97060 (503–695–2276). The ranger station is open year-round, Monday through Friday, from 8:00 A.M. to 4:30 P.M. You can also find maps at Crown Point (503–695–2240) and at Multnomah Falls Lodge.

If your visit coincides with the busy summer crush of traffic on the narrow Scenic Highway and you want to get away from the crowds, continue east toward **Ainsworth State Park.** Instead of pulling onto Interstate 84 at this point, stay to the right on the frontage road that parallels the freeway, and continue just a half-mile or so to a large parking area and the **◆Elowah Falls–McCord Creek** trailhead. Bask in the sun on large rounded rocks at the lower falls—take a left at the trail's first fork—or relax in sun-filtered shade on large rocks at the upper falls. Both hikes are easy—under 2 miles in length—and the views of the falls and gorge are spectacular, particularly on the upper falls route. These quiet, peaceful walks are far removed from the crowds and allow a focused interlude with the incredibly beautiful habitat.

If time permits, don't miss this trek into history, geology, and plant life that numerous wildlife and conservation groups are working to protect. From the Native Plant Societies of Oregon and Washington to local chapters of the Audubon Society, the Sierra Club, and the Nature Conservancy, as well as the Friends of the Columbia River Gorge, the U.S. Forest Service, the Mazamas, the Trails Club of Oregon, the American Alpine Club, and the Historic Preservation League, thousands of folks are dedicated to the task of preserving the fragile and irreplaceable as well as historical habitats within the Columbia River Gorge. For current information contact the Friends of the Columbia River Gorge, 519 SW Third Avenue (P.O. Box 40820), Portland 97240 (503–241–3762). Also ask to be sent a brochure about the annual ◆**Gorge Hiking Weekend,** which offers group hikes of various lengths and terrain in the western section of the gorge in mid-June.

Connect with Interstate 84 near McCord Creek, continuing east toward Bonneville Dam and Cascade Locks. First, detour to see ◆**Bonneville Dam,** the first hydroelectric dam constructed on the Columbia River. Built in 1937 and dedicated by President Franklin Roosevelt, the dam offers underwater views of salmon and steelhead as they swim up the fish ladders to reach the upper section of the river. There are locks for use by riverboats, a children's playground, and large shallow pools for seeing the enormous Columbia River sturgeon. These light gray, leathery-looking fish reach lengths of 5 feet and longer.

Just east of the dam, detour at Cascade Locks for a good assortment of hamburgers, soups, salads, and desserts at the **Charburger Restaurant** and enjoy a view of the Columbia River as well. In a cottonwood-shaded park along the river, just a few blocks from the restaurant, the ◆**Port of Cascade Locks Marine Park** has a small historical museum, situated in one of the original lock masters' houses, that exhibits various elements of area history. On the grounds you can also take a look at the first steam engine used on Northwest railroads. During summer the 145-foot sternwheeler *Columbia Gorge* takes visitors up and down the river from the nearby dock. For information and reservations call (503) 374–8290 or write to P.O. Box 307, Cascade Locks 97014. The telephone number in Portland is (503) 223–3928.

In 1875 army engineers recommended building a canal to circumvent the dangerous rapids at both Cascade City and The Dalles;

the work was completed in 1896. Before then passengers and cargo were unloaded and moved overland to a safer point on the river, at which location they were reloaded on a different steamboat for the continuing journey. Later, bridges connected the two sides of the Columbia River at Cascade Locks, Hood River, The Dalles, and Umatilla.

If time allows, cross the historic **Bridge of the Gods** from Cascade Locks to the Washington side of the river, turning west on Highway 14 for a few miles to **Beacon Rock.** A steep, safe trail with steps here and there leads to the top. On a bright sunny day, you can sit rather comfortably on large flat rocks atop the volcanic monolith to enjoy great views of the gorge upriver to the east and downriver to the west.

For an extra, visual treat, return east on Highway 14, continue a couple of miles beyond the bridge toward Stevenson, turning north in just a quarter mile or so to visit the new **Skamania Lodge.** It overlooks the gorge to the east, on the Washington side of the Columbia River. The rustic Cascadian-style lodge (with its enormous fireplace lobby-lounge) offers overnight accommodations, an 18-hole golf course, tennis courts, walking and horseback-riding trails, a gift shop, an indoor swimming pool and a natural rock outdoor whirlpool spa, meeting rooms, and a lovely restaurant and lounge that both take advantage of all that marvelous scenery. For information and reservations the toll-free telephone number is (800) 221–7117. To arrange guided horseback rides, contact Dundee and Sally Dudley at Columbia Gorge Outfitters, P.O. Box 935, Stevenson, Washington 98648 (509–427–8371 or 509–427–7700). Notice, too, whether or not the new **Columbia Gorge Interpretive Center** is open; it is located just below the lodge and also commands a grand view of the river and gorge toward the east. For current hours and information, call the staff at Skamania County Museum, (509) 427–5141, extension 235.

Return to the Oregon side and Interstate 84 via Bridge of the Gods, heading east again. Detour at Hood River, about 8 miles east of Cascade Locks, and wind down to the **Hood River Boat Basin and Marina Park** to watch dozens of men and women ply the Columbia's rough waters on sailboards that sport sails of bright rainbow colors. This particularly windy stretch of the river between Cascade Locks, Hood River, The Dalles, and Rufus has become, within the past several years, a mecca for the intrepid sailboarders. With their oblong boards firmly attached

Sailboarding on Hood River

atop cars and vans, these enthusiasts return like flocks of migrating birds, beginning in April and remaining through September.

You may want to stop at the well-stocked Hood River Visitors' Information Center, located near the marina, for current maps and local tourist information, or write ahead to the center's mailing address: Port Marina Park, Hood River 97031 (503–386–2000). Helpful information and brochures can also be obtained from the Columbia River Gorge National Scenic Area, Wacoma Center, 902 Wasco Avenue, Hood River 97031 (503–386–2333).

For a glimpse into Hood River's interesting past, plan to visit the **Hood River County Museum**—also located near Port Marina Park—where exhibits of Native American culture, pioneer history, lumbering, and fruit-growing memorabilia are displayed. The museum is open May through October, Wednesday through Saturday from 10:00 A.M. to 4:00 P.M. and Sunday from noon to 4:00 P.M. Call (503) 386–4547 for additional information.

Speaking of fruit, if travels bring you to the area in early spring, plan to take in the annual **Hood River Valley Blossom Festival** during the third weekend of April, when thousands of pear, apple, and cherry trees are in glorious bloom in the Hood River Valley. Local tours through the orchards, along with arts-and-crafts fairs, quilt sales, antiques sales, and open houses at fruit-packing establishments, wineries, and fire departments, are among the eclectic round of activities that take place throughout the weekend.

One of the best offerings is a nostalgic train ride on the **Mt. Hood Railroad**'s Fruit Blossom Special, which winds through the flowering orchards to Parkdale and Odell. The old railroad, which began in 1906 as a passenger and freight line, was resurrected in 1987, when a group of enterprising Hood River–area citizens purchased it from the Union Pacific Railroad. Several circa 1910–26 Pullman coaches have been restored and are pulled by two General Motors/EMD GP-9 locomotives built in the 1950s. The Mt. Hood Railroad Depot in downtown Hood River, built in 1911, was completely refurbished as well and has won a National Historic Site designation.

The summer excursions begin during the Blossom Festival weekend, and there is often a Christmas Tree Express in December. The round-trip between Hood River and Parkdale takes four and a half hours, including an hour's layover at lovely Woodworth Park; the Odell excursion takes two hours and makes just a fifteen-minute stop. For additional information contact the Mt. Hood Railroad, 110 Railroad Avenue, Hod River 97031 (503–386–3556).

For overnight accommodations check with the friendly folks at the refurbished ◆**Hood River Hotel,** located near the railroad depot. After a year of intensive renovation (the empty old hotel was purchased by Canadian sailboarder Pasquale Barone), the four-story red brick structure has reopened its doors to Columbia River Gorge travelers.

Forest-green carpeting with touches of coral replaces old checkerboard tiles, and graceful, Queen Anne–style furniture upholstered in soft teal, green, and cream replaces the prim, overstuffed mohair chairs and settees of 1913. The hotel was built as an annex to the circa 1890 Mt. Hood Hotel, which was razed in 1920. Now awakened from its slumber, the light-filled old dowager today offers an Old World European charm and twenty-six refurbished guest rooms. Guests sleep in elegant canopied or four-poster beds; the bureaus and dressing tables are made of polished cherry; bleached fir floors, pier-glass mirrors, and colorful chintzes complete the new decor.

Breakfast, lunch, and dinner are available in the hotel restaurant, open daily from 7:00 A.M. to 10:00 P.M.; guests are served a continental breakfast. For further information and reservations, contact the Hood River Hotel, 102 Oak Street, Hood River 97031 (503–386–1900).

If you decide to detour from Hood River south toward Parkdale and the Mt. Hood Recreation Area, the **Coffee Spot,** located at 12 Oak Street, is a good place to stop for made-to-order deli sandwiches, salads, soups, and special desserts. The restaurant is open Monday through Friday from 8:00 A.M. to 5:30 P.M. and Saturday from 9:00 A.M. to 4:00 P.M.

You might head instead into the eastern section of the Columbia River Gorge to attend a second, equally popular spring festival that takes place just 21 miles east of Hood River, in The Dalles. The **Northwest Cherry Festival** is celebrated during the third week of April, from Monday through Saturday, and culminates with the Festival Parade on Saturday morning at 11:00 A.M. Equestrian units, Native Americans, local marching bands, and colorful clowns wind through the historic downtown area.

Another good spot for watching those intriguing sailboarders, along with a bevy of ducks and geese, is ◆**The Dalles Boat Basin Beach,** where there is protected onshore wind most of the time, a minimal river current, and no barge traffic. Historically this portion of the Columbia River Gorge, at The Dalles, was the end of the arduous, 2,000-mile trail for those first Oregon-bound pioneers in 1843. At this location the families and their heavy wagons were loaded aboard makeshift barges and floated down the swift river some 80 miles to the site of Fort Vancouver, near the confluence of the Columbia and Willamette rivers.

Explorers Lewis and Clark, as well as the French fur trappers and native peoples who preceded them, also knew intimately the river and its swift currents. They navigated its rapids and 4- to 6-foot waves in dugouts hand-hewn from large Douglas fir trunks. The mighty Columbia River, whose humble beginnings are traced north to the Canadian Rockies in British Columbia, has been tamed for both navigation and flood control by a series of power-generating dams. Over the years many of those dams obliterated both the historic rapids and the ancient fishing grounds of native peoples. An example is the famous Celilo Falls, which were near the site of **The Dalles Dam.** For centuries the Indians fished from rocky basalt ledges on this stretch of the river, and later they fished from spindly wooden "scaffolding" affairs near the falls, catching the large salmon with long-poled nets.

For information about visiting the dam or attending the festival, contact The Dalles Area Visitors' Information Center, 901 E. Second Street, The Dalles 97058 (503–296–6616). Also inquire about other interesting festivals, such as the Celilo Wyam Salmon Feast in early April, the Tygh Valley All Indian Rodeo in mid-May, the Fort Dalles Rodeo in mid-July, the historic Dufur Threshing Bee in early August, the Gorge Cities Windsurfing Blowout in mid-August, and the Wasco County Fair at the end of August.

To better understand the vital historical significance of this area, make a visit to the **Fort Dalles Historical Museum,** at Sixteenth and Garrison, set in the only remaining building of 1856 Fort Dalles. The Carpenter Gothic structure is listed on the National Register of Historic Places, and the museum is open May through September on Tuesday through Friday from 10:30 A.M. to 5:00 P.M. and on Saturday and Sunday from 10:00 A.M. to 5:00 P.M.; hours from October to April 1 are limited, usually from noon to 4:00 P.M. Call (503) 296–6616 for information.

Ask, too, about the self-guided walking or driving tour of historic homes and buildings and for directions to lovely **Sorosis Park,** located above the city and offering a viewing spot and a rose garden at the top of the bluff. From the viewing area notice the large bend in the Columbia River. By the point where the river reaches The Dalles, the Douglas fir–clothed western section of the gorge has changed to another elevation, above 2,000 feet, to the sunny eastern high desert. Now the rounded, hunched hills are sparsely clad, and in nearby canyons, sagebrush and bitterbrush bloom splashes of yellow in the spring and early summer. Rolling wheat country extends east and north of The Dalles up into Wasco, Moro, and Grass Valley, and thousands of cherry trees blossom in nearby orchards as well.

You can stop at **Dobre Deli,** located downtown at 308 E. Fourth Street,for sandwiches, freshly made salads and soups, and desserts. The deli is open Monday through Friday from 8:00 A.M. to 8:00 P.M. and Saturday from 9:00 A.M. to 5:00 P.M. Call (503) 298–8239 for further information.

Then call ahead to see if innkeepers Don and Barbara Williams have guest rooms available at the historic **Williams House Bed and Breakfast Inn,** located at 608 W. Sixth Street, The Dalles 97058. The gingerbread-trimmed Victorian mansion was constructed by a local judge in 1899, fifty-six years after the first families trekked across the dusty Oregon Trail from Independence, Missouri. The elegant home has been in the Williams family since 1926. For information and reservations contact the innkeepers at (503) 296–2889.

From The Dalles take another pleasant side trip into history, the rural past, by heading south on Highway 197 just 13 miles to the tiny farming community of **Dufur.** You're definitely in the slow lane now. Gently rolling wheat fields, the color of honey, extend for miles and miles in all four directions. Several tall grain elevators punctuate the wide blue skyline. You see Mt. Hood's snowy peak to the west. There is no freeway noise, just quantities of fresh, clean air and friendly smiles from local residents. You ease into the rhythm of the farmland, and you aren't bothered by the fact that there is only one place to stay overnight in Dufur, the **Balch Hotel.** You don't mind that your room has neither television nor telephone.

Pat and Howard Green bought Charley Balch's circa 1907 rundown, brick hotel in 1986 and have spent the last several years bringing it, and twenty-one guest rooms, back to life. In the early 1900s wealthy stockmen, loggers and rough farmhands, and women in long, black dresses walked through the doors of the hostelry that was an elegant showpiece at the end of the Great Southern Railroad line. Lodging is offered most weekends; the renovation is still ongoing. Full meals aren't served yet, but you'll get a delicious continental breakfast, and there are two restaurants within walking distance. For information and reservations contact the Greens at P.O. Box 5, Dufur 97021, or call (503) 467–2277. Ask, too, about the annual Dufur Threshing Bee.

MT. HOOD RECREATION AREA

Mt. Hood, an imposing, snow-covered, andesite volcano rising some 11,235 feet from the forested Cascades, easily dominates the skyline to the south of Hood River and is always seen on clear days from Portland, 50 miles to the west. Newcomers, as well as those of us who have lived in Portland and in the Columbia River Gorge area most of our lives, all naturally claim the mountain as our personal property.

One of the most scenic routes to the mountain is accessed from Hood River at the exit near Port Marina Park. Along Highway 35 you'll encounter the venerable, snowcapped peak around many bends while winding up through the Hood River Valley's lush orchards. When driving through the area in the fall, detour at **Sappington Orchards** to sample fresh apple cider and purchase homemade applesauce and gift packages of delicious apples and pears from orchardists Bill and Betty Sappington. The orchards are located at 3187 Highway 35, about 6 miles from Hood River; visitors are welcome to stop from September 15 to December 15 daily, between 9:00 A.M. and 6:00 P.M. Call (503) 386–3357 for additional information.

Legend passed down by native peoples says that Mt. Hood was at one time a mighty volcano known as Wy'east, a great chief turned into a mountain, spouting flame and hurling boulders skyward in anger. The first recorded white people, members of the British Royal Navy, saw the mountain in 1792 from their vessel, sailing on the Columbia River. A British naval officer named it Hood, after his admiral. The earliest whites to trek over the slopes of Mt. Hood were most likely French fur trappers, in about 1818; botanist David Douglas, in 1833; and a few other hardy souls who followed the main deer and Indian trails connecting the east and west sides of the mountain.

For a good bit of history and a helpful map of the first emigrant road across the Cascades along those ancient Indian trails, pick up a copy of *The Barlow Road,* available from the Mt. Hood National Forest Office, 2955 NW Division Street, Gresham 97030 (503–666–0700); or stop at the Hood River Ranger Station near Parkdale, on Highway 35; the phone number is (503) 352–6002 or toll-free from Portland, (800) 223–4590.

A great place to eat along this route is at **Cooper Spur Inn,** located at 10755 Cooper Spur Road, about 23 miles from Hood River. Sitting snugly on the eastern flank of Mt. Hood, this log cabin–style steakhouse is noted for serving logger-style portions of food, plus its comfortable and rustic mountain atmosphere. The inn is open daily from 9:00 A.M. to 9:00 P.M. For dinner reservations telephone the staff at (503) 352-6037. Incidentally, the **Cooper Spur Ski Area,** just up the road from the inn, is an especially good place for families and beginners to enjoy skiing without scores of hotdog snowboarders, who tend to take over the slopes at times. Here you'll encounter just 500 vertical feet of terrain on about one hundred skiable acres with two surface ski lifts. For information call (503) 352-7803. Another good area for beginners is at **Summit Ski Area** in Government Camp; there is also a good inner-tubing hill for the kids here. The telephone number is (503) 272–0256.

The **Barlow Road,** opened in 1845, completed the Oregon Trail as a land route from Independence, Missouri, to the Willamette Valley. This alternate land route to Oregon City on the Willamette River became a major entry into western Oregon for those who wanted to avoid the dangers or costs of floating down the Columbia River from The Dalles to Fort Vancouver.

Samuel K. Barlow, his family, and others literally chopped the crude wagon trail through the thick evergreen forest on the southeast and southwest flanks of the mountain to a location between Government Camp and Rhododendron. Following roughly the same route, Highway 35 intersects with Highway 26 just south of the **Mt. Hood Meadows Ski Area,** turning west about 6 miles to historic Government Camp. (You can also head east at this point, toward Kah-Nee-Ta and central Oregon.)

On the way to Government Camp, stop to see remnants of the Barlow Trail and **Summit Meadows,** where the immigrants camped, near **Trillium Lake.** The Forest Service access road, from Highway 26, is just opposite the **Snow Bunny Ski Area**—a great place for families with small children—a few miles west of the Highway 35 junction. Near the large meadow are a small pioneer cemetery and the site of one of the early tollhouses, Summit House. Notice the many pioneer names scratched into the surface of nearby boulders—perhaps to notify the next contingent of immigrants scheduled to arrive.

At this site stood Perry Vicker's log cabin, barn, lodge, and shingled teepee. Vickers also built, across the north edge of the meadows, a corduroy road—a type of early road constructed by laying small tree trunks side by side. Such roads became familiar surfaces for horse-drawn wagons and, later, for the first automobiles. Needless to say, traveling in those early days was a distinct challenge and more often than not included moving branches, or even fallen trees, off the roadway in order to continue the journey. One's basic travel equipment included both axes and handsaws, as well as extra water for refilling radiators that often "boiled over" on steep mountain roads.

Hike or drive down to Trillium Lake for a picnic and stay in one of the nearby campgrounds: one right on the lake and the other, **Still Creek Campground,** along the creek just north of the pioneer graves and Summit Meadows. During July and August you'll probably find delicious huckleberries along Still Creek; during winter you'll want to clamp on cross-country skis and trek across the snowy meadow and onto the same roads all the way around the frozen lake.

In historic Government Camp sleep snug and warm at **Falcon's Crest Inn,** at an elevation of 4,000 feet and imagine what sleeping outdoors in a covered wagon might have been like. Good-natured innkeepers Bob and Melody Johnson pamper guests with special treats, the sort those emigrants probably never experienced at Perry Vickers's tollgate cabin just up the road at Summit Meadows. Try evening aperitifs and appetizers served in the comfortable Great Room, warmed by an enormous wood stove; then a supper, if you wish, a prix fixe affair; and finally a morning tray, set just outside your door, of steaming-hot coffee and freshly baked muffins, often with both orange and cranberry butters. Breakfast at the dining table, with its ample window views, may consist of waffles with a strawberry compote, a special mushroom quiche, or a cheesy omelet, along with fresh seasonal fruits, juices, and coffee or herbal teas.

During winter guests can ski at the nearby **Ski Bowl**; sleigh rides can sometimes be arranged, and you can enjoy the inn's holiday decor. (Doesn't everyone have seven lighted and decorated Christmas trees?) During summer go hiking on nearby trails into roadside areas or alpine meadows filled with white bear grass, red-orange Indian paintbrush, blue lupine, pale pink native rhododendrons, white and pink foxglove, red elderberry, and many other native plants, depending on the season. For the particulars and for reservations, contact Bob and Melody Johnson at Falcon's Crest Inn, P.O. Box 185, Government Camp 97028 (503–272–3403).

In the early 1900s pioneer guide Oliver Yocum built a hotel at Government Camp, and it survived until 1933, when a fire destroyed it. Within 10 years after the Barlows' pioneering route over the shoulder of Mt. Hood, the mountain became a much-sought-after landmark, instead of a formidable nuisance, and for more than a century and a half it has drawn city dwellers to its slopes year-round.

As early as 1890 skiers and climbers flocked to the snowy slopes of Mt. Hood. In those days their journey was substantial, involving several days' travel to get from Portland to the mountain. Until a graded road was constructed to Government Camp in the 1920s, the last day's trek during winter months was via snowshoes from Rhododendron. In 1924 the first hotel at timberline was built by the Forest Service, near the present Timberline Lodge. Serving as emergency shelter during summer and winter, the original lodge was about 8 by 16 feet, with several additional tents nearby. You brought your own blankets, rented a mattress, and got a meal.

Today travelers can sleep in more luxurious comfort at this 6,000-foot level by checking in at one of the state's oldest mountain inns, ◆ **Timberline Lodge,** located just 6 miles up the mountain from Government Camp. Construction of the lodge was approved in 1935 by President Franklin Roosevelt as a project of the Works Progress Administration during the Great Depression. A contingent of more than 250 Northwest artisans—

carpenters, stonemasons, woodcarvers, metalworkers, painters, weavers, and furniture makers—created in two years a magnificent lodge that looks like the rough-hewn castle of a legendary Norse mountain king.

The lodge was dedicated by President Roosevelt in September 1937 and officially opened to the public in February 1938. Fires crackled in the massive fireplaces—hexagonal, 14 feet in diameter, constructed with 400 tons of native stone, and rising 92 feet in the peak, six fire pits in all—as a parade of some 150 guests registered for the opening weekend. Today you can hear FDR's voice crackling from a vintage recording—a portion of his dedication speech—as you walk through the **Rachel Griffen Historic Exhibition Center** on the refurbished main-entry level.

Just imagine, however, in the not-too-distant past, us skiers grouped about those massive entry-level fireplaces drying our ski socks and munching sack lunches before heading back to the snowy slopes. Nowadays skiers use the new Wy'east Day Lodge, just across the upper parking area, and this practice does, of course, greatly protect the original lodge, which often logs more than a million visitors each year.

Most of the fifty-nine guest rooms are one of a kind, with carved headboards, patchwork quilts, and hooked rugs. Everything was made by hand—some of the original curtains, from dying old army uniforms and blankets. The original fabrics and weavings, along with the Native American, pioneer, native wildflower, and animal motifs, have all been restored and repaired through the painstaking efforts of the **Friends of Timberline.** Above the second-floor lounge and restaurant is a quaint, hexagonal-shaped balcony with small alcoves, some with benches and desks offering a place to write letters or read. To the north, floor-to-ceiling windows frame spectacular Mt. Hood.

For information about year-round activities and events, and for reservations, contact the staff at Timberline Lodge, Government Camp 97028 (503–231–7979). The manager is longtime mountain lover Richard Kohnstamm.

According to historical records the first people to actually climb Mt. Hood, on July 11, 1857, were members of a party led by Henry L. Pittock, who published the *Oregonian* newspaper; in 1876, the first females to climb to the summit were two women wearing traditional Victorian long skirts.

Another notable mountaineer, Elijah Coalman, first climbed Mt. Hood at age fifteen, in 1897. He later became the first fire lookout on top of the mountain, in 1914, and in 1915 he built the first shelter at the summit. Elijah must have thrived on deep snow, chilling winds, and icy crevasses, for he climbed Mt. Hood nearly 600 times and stayed on as lookout until 1930.

In the early 1940s the state highway commission decided upon a great experiment: to keep the section of narrow road between Welches and Government Camp open throughout the entire winter. Winter sports enthusiasts were exhilarated. They flocked to the mountain, and the pilgrimage to Mt. Hood has never ceased. For information about alpine and Nordic skiing areas, as well as the names of expert instructors and mountain-climbing guides, contact the **Mt. Hood Recreation Association,** 68260 E. Welches Road, Welches 97067 (503–622–3017). *Note:* Do not entertain the notion of climbing Mt. Hood—or any other mountain in the high Cascades—without expert guidance, preparation, and assistance.

From mid-July through September during the late 1870s, a wagon with a good team of horses could make a pleasant trip from Portland to Government Camp in two and a half to three days. Some families camped there the entire summer, enjoying warm mountain breezes and dining on such delicacies as mountain huckleberries, blackberries, and fish from near-by streams.

If you visit the **Mt. Hood Recreation Area** from July through September—summer on the mountain—use your copy of *The Barlow Road,* which has a clearly marked map, along with a copy of the Mt. Hood National Forest map, and explore to your heart's content on well-marked Forest Service roads. Both maps can be obtained at the Zig Zag Ranger Station, just below Toll Gate Campground and Rhododendron, Highway 26, Zig Zag 97049 (503–622–3191).

While you're there, ask for current information about summer and fall day hikes in the area. In the nearby **Salmon Huckleberry Wilderness** is the easily accessed **Salmon River National Recreation Trail.** The Salmon River Gorge, with its many waterfalls, is a picturesque area of volcanic plugs, pinnacles, and forested cliffs. The trail lies several hundred feet above the river, except for the lower 2½-mile section.

Ask for directions to the **Hidden Lake Trail,** located just 6 miles east of the Zig Zag Ranger Station. The trail is accessed from a side road at the bottom of Laurel Hill (imagine the pioneers' back-breaking struggle in negotiating their heavy wagons down this steep precipice, using long ropes). In early to mid-June you'll find the lakeside section of the trail punctuated with masses of pale pink blooms from the stately native rhododendrons.

In addition, the 2-mile **Mountaineer Trail,** located higher on the mountain, is an especially good hike for families. Passable from August through October, this trail is found on the east side of Timberline Lodge and climbs through gnarled alpine fir beyond the timberline to **Silcox Hut,** at the 7,000-foot level. You'll have splendid panoramic views of Mt. Jefferson, Three Sisters, and Broken Top to the south and east and, on a clear day, of the Coast Range some 85 miles to the west. The trail, though steep in some places, is easy to navigate and takes about two hours round-trip.

If you decide to take a snack or a picnic along on your mountain hikes, stop at **Northwest Deli** in Welches before leaving the Zig Zag area and heading east, climbing toward Laurel Hill, Government Camp, or Timberline. Hearty sandwiches, delicious homemade soups, and marvelous cinnamon rolls, together with a selection of imported beers and regional wines, are available here Monday through Saturday. Located in the minimall next to the Thriftway Grocery, the Deli also serves breakfast and lunch.

For handmade gifts and willow furniture along with note cards, candles, and casual sportswear, stop and snoop through the many treasures offered by Susie Welch at **Heart of the Mountain Gifts and Treasures.** Her charming gift shop is located at 67898 East Highway 26 in Welches (503–622–3451). Susie usually has gourmet coffees and teas to try as well, and she offers personalized gift wrapping, too. Her hours are noon to 5:00 P.M. on Sundays and 10:00 A.M. to 6:00 P.M. all other days except Tuesdays, when the shop is closed.

For a delicious supper pull over at **Don Guidos Restaurant** in Rhododendron, just a few miles down the mountain from Government Camp. New owners Doug and Anne Kinne have renovated the interior of the old Log Lodge, long known to skiers and mountain dwellers. Notice the walls of large polished logs with their original horsehair chinking. The place has a warm, inviting atmosphere, and the Kinnes especially welcome families. They and their friendly staff (Don does much of the gourmet cooking) serve Italian-style entrées such as eggplant Renee, seafood cannelloni, chicken piccata, and veal Marsala. Call ahead for dinner reservations at (503) 622–5141. Ask about the new espresso bar, where you can stop for piping hot Caffe Latte, Cafe Americano, and Cafe Mocha as well as cold Italian sodas and a variety of gourmet pastries. The restaurant is open for dinner from 5:30 to 10:00 P.M. every day except Mondays.

Since bedding down at lower elevations may be just as appealing as sleeping in the clouds, consider ◆ **Old Welches Bed and Breakfast Inn,** located just below Zig Zag on Welches Road—turn south at the stoplight—just across from the old front 9 of the original Bowman's Resort (now a classy resort, with the golf course expanded to 36 holes). Judi Mondun and her family have restored Jennie Welch's lovely home, and Judy especially welcomes bed-and-breakfast travelers who appreciate a sense of history.

Sunlight fills the old home, which at one time was an inn that welcomed those early Portlanders who came to the mountain during summer to camp, fish, and pick gallons of juicy blackberries and huckleberries. Light, airy guest rooms on the second floor offer old-fashioned prints, comfortable sitting places, and queen-size beds. Breakfast is served in the spacious dining room just off the kitchen and the French doors that open to the outside patio and garden. The Salmon River bubbles quietly just beyond, and you can walk a short path for a close-up view. For reservations contact Judi Mondun at Old Welches Bed and Breakfast Inn, 26401 East Welches Road, Welches 97067 (503–622–3754).

Farther down the mountain via Highway 26 toward Sandy, the **Ivy Bear Restaurant** has reopened, offering Old World cuisine in a comfortable atmosphere. Serving dinners on Tuesday through Sunday from 4:00 to 10:00 P.M., the restaurant features such tasty items as Bohemian sauerbraten, Hungarian goulash, pasta carbonara, and Hunter veal, along with Crème Caramel Kahlua and special fruit crepes for dessert. The restaurant is located at 54735 East Highway 26, between Sandy and Welches; its phone number is (503) 622–3440.

Summer visitors can take in **Sandy Mountain Days,** held in the community of Sandy, just down the mountain from Welches and Brightwood, toward Gresham. Highlighting the mid-July festival are, in addition to a carnival and parade, the international Bed Race finals, a wine fair and feast, and a gathering of about 150 Northwest artists and craftspersons who display, demonstrate, and sell their wares in shady **Meining Memorial Park.**

You can enjoy live melodrama and variety shows in the park's Birdcage Theater, as well as every kind of music—from bluegrass and western to big-band sounds. Visitors are invited to "come as you are or dress in old-fashioned gingham or buckskin." The annual Black Powder Shoot, also held during the festival, is patterned after the rendezvous of those early trappers who came out of the mountains once a year to trade their furs and "whoop it up." You can see demonstrations of old-fashioned black powder shooting and of knife and tomahawk throwing, as well as participate in rifle trail walks. The rendezvous is family oriented, with some black powder shooters, dressed in miniature buckskins, as young as six years old.

While visiting Meining Memorial Park, stroll through the lovely garden designed for the blind; it contains a variety of scented herbs and an assortment of perennials and annuals of different textures.

For additional information and a helpful brochure about the festival and the park, write to the Sandy Visitors' Information Center, P.O. Box 536, Sandy 97055, or call (503) 668–4006.

The Willamette Valley

Farms and Vineyards

Heart of the Valley

Salem

Eugene

Covered Bridge Country

Central Cascades

1. Champoeg State Park
2. Helvetia Tavern
3. Draft-Horse Plowing Exhibition
4. Montinore Vineyards
5. Ballad Town U.S.A.
6. Trolley Park Museum
7. Flying M Ranch
8. Lafayette Schoolhouse Antiques Mall
9. Steiger Haus Bed and Breakfast
10. Wheatland Ferry
11. Mission Mill Village
12. Bush House and Deepwood Estate Gardens
13. Marquee House Bed and Breakfast
14. Mt. Angel Abbey
15. Albany Historic Districts
16. Avery Park and Rose Gardens
17. William L. Finley National Wildlife Refuge
18. Euphoria Chocolate Company
19. Starbuck's Coffee House
20. Canoeing on the Millrace
21. Black Bart Bed and Breakfast
22. Dorris Ranch
23. McKenzie Pass Scenic Drive
24. Dee Wright Observatory
25. Belknap Springs Lodge
26. McKenzie River Driftboats
27. Salt Creek Falls
28. Odell Lake Lodge
29. Red Bridge
30. June Mountain Trail

The Willamette Valley

Farms and Vineyards

Eons old, with rivers meandering through and bisecting its green hills and rich alluvial soils, the Willamette Valley was surely a welcome sight to the weary pioneers fresh off the Oregon Trail. Out of those abundant soils grew many farms in the 1840s and 1850s and, much later, the hundreds of orchards, nurseries, and vineyards that continue to thrive in this moist and mild zone between the high Cascade and lower Coast Range mountains and the Pacific Ocean.

This gentle region, now scattered with cities, towns, hamlets, and inviting side roads that skirt Interstate 5 and old Highways 99E and 99W, was also home to the Calapooya Indians. For thousands of years they roamed throughout the broad valley, digging tiny bulbs of the purple camas in early spring, picking juicy blackberries in late summer, and hunting deer and fishing its rivers and streams nearly year-round. If you visit in mid-May, you'll see waves of purple camas blooming along roadsides in meadows throughout the valley.

To get acquainted with this large region, which lies like an enormous green carpet between the mountains and the ocean, first head south from Portland on Interstate 5 past Wilsonville to **Champoeg State Park.** This historic, 567-acre park preserves the site of the May 2, 1843, meeting at which valley settlers, by a narrow vote, established the first organized territorial government in the Northwest. George Abernethy was elected the territory's first governor. Champoeg was later an important stagecoach stop, trading post, and port for steamboats plying the upper and lower sections of the Willamette River—until the late 1880s, when the small settlement, like many others along the banks of the river, was destroyed by flood.

In July and August you can take in an annual outdoor drama at the park, *Champoeg: The Story of Old Oregon,* depicting the region's history. The historic meeting at Champoeg climaxes the drama's first act; the second act includes bits about the Oregon Trail and the political struggle between the United States and Great Britain for control of the territory. Troubled relations between Indian tribes and settlers, the Whitman Massacre, and the constitutional debates leading to statehood are also dramatized in the updated script by Charles Deemer, a regional playwright.

Sponsored by the Friends of Champoeg in cooperation with the Oregon State Parks and Recreation Division, the outdoor drama runs Tuesday through Saturday during summer, beginning at 7:30 P.M. Tickets can be purchased at the gate or by callling (503) 657–0988. The Champoeg Visitors' Center exhibit area is open year-round, and the park offers picnicking, biking, hiking, and camping.

Before continuing south toward the state capital, meander over to **Newberg, McMinnville,** and **Forest Grove** to see where many of the old orchards were planted, where new fields of wine grapes are taking root, and where fine old homes are living new lives as tasting rooms or bed-and-breakfast inns. Hundreds of acres are planted with premium wine grapes, and scores of small wineries process the fruit into more than 100,000 gallons of vinifera wines and into thousands of gallons of premium fruit and berry wines. With helpful maps, strike out on your own to visit many wineries and tasting rooms.

To plan a self-guided tour, pick up the handy map at the Washington County Visitors' Association, 10172 SW Washington Square Road (503–684–5555), located in Washington Square, just off the Greenberg Road exit from Highway 217, near Beaverton. The locations of these wineries and vineyards range from Beaverton and Newberg out to Hillsboro and Forest Grove. Ask, too, for a copy of the annual *Discover Oregon Wineries,* containing detailed maps for visiting vineyards throughout the state.

If you head out toward the Hillsboro area from Portland or Beaverton, plan to stop at the **Helvetia Tavern,** located on Helvetia Road just beyond where the road dips under the railroad trestle, about 2 miles north of the Sunset Highway (Highway 26). Your reward for finding this local gem will be hamburgers the size of dinner plates and fresh-cooked french fries—with skins left on—piled all around. Watch the folks play pool, or join in yourself. And notice the interesting collection of hats hanging from the walls and rafters. The tavern is open for lunch and dinner every day; its phone number is (503) 647–5286. *Note:* The gentle back roads in this area are fine for bicycling, as well; ask about bike maps at the Washington County Visitors' Association.

If the notion of gargantuan burgers sounds too much for lunch, backtrack on the Sunset Highway a couple of miles and exit at Cornelius Pass for a lunch or dinner stop at the historic 1866 Imbrie Farmstead. It's been transformed into a restaurant and microbrewery, the **Cornelius Pass Roadhouse.** At the exit head south just a short distance to the restored, two-story Victorian, with its large front porch and balcony. The roadhouse is open for lunch and dinner every day, from 11:00 A.M. to 10:00 P.M. Call (503) 640–6174 for more information.

Farms are a way of life in the Willamette Valley, where the passing of the four seasons signals familiar chores having to do with plowing, planting, growing, and harvesting. One group of dedicated draft plowmen, members of the Oregon Draft Horse Breeders Association, continue efforts to improve the five major draft-horse breeds still used for plowing in many areas of the United States. Each spring they, along with the Washington County Historical Society and local service organizations, sponsor the annual **Draft-Horse Plowing Exhibition.**

At the historical society's center, on the Rock Creek Campus of Portland Community College, you can watch some twenty teams of draft horses (and draft mules) in three-horse teams, each with one plow, demonstrate disk harrowing and plowing. All major breeds of the gentle giants are represented, including Belgian, Clydesdale, Percheron, Suffolk, and Shire. Sets of harness used 150 years ago and brought to the territory over the Oregon Trail are used with several of the teams.

Park the car and ride horse-drawn hay wagons to the re-created 1889 farmstead exhibition area, where both you and the kids can watch demonstrations of blacksmithing, harnessing, shoeing, and wheelwrighting, as well as plowing. Bring a picnic lunch or purchase fried chicken, barbecued beef, hamburgers, desserts, and beverages at the farmstead village. The exhibition is held the third Saturday in May, from 10:00 A.M. to 4:00 P.M., near the Washington County Historical Museum on the college campus at 17705 NW Springville Road, just north of the Sunset Highway turning off Highway 26 at the 185th Avenue exit; call (503) 645–5353 for further information.

Next throw a corkscrew into the picnic basket and head west on Highway 8 from Hillsboro to Forest Grove, detouring south on Highway 47 to trek farther off the vineyard-visiting path. Here the vineyards—many have tasting rooms and paths to stroll, offering great views of the valley and mountains—nestle closer to the foothills of the Coast Range mountains, patchwork-quilting the gently rolling hills with rows of such grapes as chardonnays, Rieslings, and Pinot noirs. The Pinot noir is a fussy, temperamental grape that grows especially well at this elevation.

You can visit one of the newest and most elegant tasting rooms at **Montinore Vineyards,** where you'll most likely sip a Pinot noir, chardonnay, white Riesling, chenin blanc, or gewürztraminer, with outstanding views and soft music from an antique square grand piano for company. The vineyard is located on Dilley Road just 2 miles south of Forest Grove via Highway 47; call (503) 359–5012. This impressive, 588-acre wine estate is located near the Washington–Yamhill County border.

Incidentally, Forest Grove is known as **Ballad Town U.S.A.,** where championship barbershop quartets raise melodious voices in old-fashioned harmony each year in mid-March. The tickets disappear like hotcakes, and so for current information, you'll want early to contact the Forest Grove Visitors' Information Center, 2417 Pacific Avenue, Forest Grove 97116 (503–357–3006). In addition, pick up another helpful map for self-guided trips to more vineyards from the Yamhill County Wineries Association, P.O. Box 871, McMinnville 97128 (503–434–5814).

Keep in mind that the back roads into vineyards and wineries are often narrow, lack shoulders, and sometimes change from paved to gravel in the hinterlands. Both farm equipment and straying cows can be encountered along the way, and locals tend to drive somewhat faster than visitors. Look for places to pull off the road completely, and then walk back to viewing areas. Sturdy walking shoes and umbrellas are also helpful to have along in case of dusty roads or showers.

Just west of Forest Grove, at the 38-mile post on Highway 6, climb into an old-time trolley for a ride into **Trolley Park Museum** to see a collection of trolleys, double-deckers and interurbans that have been restored by the **Oregon Electric Railway Historical Society.** Access Highway 6 from Forest Grove via Highway 8, turning toward Tillamook at the junction. The park is open to visitors from May through October on weekends and holidays. Call (503) 357–3574 for more information.

While rambling through the rolling Yamhill County area,

and if time allows, plan dinner and western-style dancing at the ◆ **Flying M Ranch,** located in the Coast Range foothills near Trask Mountain, just west of the historic community of Yamhill. Rebuilt after a disastrous fire by owners Bryce and Barbara Mitchell, the 17,000-square-foot main lodge is constructed of enormous logs, many of them from the ranch property. In the dining area relax at polished hand-hewn tables and chairs grouped around the large stone fireplace that survived the fire. In the lounge sit by large windows and spy deer as they cross the North Yamhill River, bubbling below; or belly up to the 30-foot-long bar, constructed from a Douglas fir trunk that, when felled, was 36 inches across. The hand-carved bar weighs about six tons.

Bryce is a logger, and Barbara manages the inn—the ranch has a motel-bunkhouse offering overnight accommodations—and both Mitchells love horses; more than fifty head graze in the lower pastures. Overnight trail rides, complete with hearty meals cooked outdoors, are featured during summer months. If you're a small-aircraft enthusiast, you could fly in for lunch or dinner, using the ranch's 2,200-foot grass airstrip; fuel is available at the Newberg and McMinnville airports.

The restaurant is open for breakfast, lunch, and dinner Monday through Thursday from 8:00 A.M. to 8:00 P.M. and Friday through Sunday from 8:00 A.M. to 10:00 P.M. (except December 24–25). The ranch is 10 miles west of Yamhill; follow the FLYING M signs to 23029 NW Flying M Road. The facilities also include campsites for tents and recreational vehicles along the river, as well as several cabins with kitchens. For reservations and more information, call (503) 662–3222.

From Yamhill take Highway 47 south to Highway 99W and detour west to McMinnville, the largest community in the Tualatin Valley.

Lovers of antiques can easily find the nearby community of Lafayette and poke through eight classrooms filled with treasures and memorabilia of all kinds, sizes, and shapes at the ◆ **Lafayette Schoolhouse Antiques Mall.** Housed in the circa 1910 school building at 748 Third Street (Highway 99W), the mall is billed as the state's "largest permanent antique show," a place where some ninety entrepreneurs display their wares—from porcelain, china, glassware, and pottery to dolls, linens, vintage clothing, and furniture. The mall is open every day from 10:00 A.M. to 5:00 P.M.; the phone number is (503) 864–2720.

If you'd like to stay overnight near the antiques and wine country, call Doris and Lynn Steiger at ◆**Steiger Haus Bed and Breakfast,** friendly folks who offer Old World–style hospitality in a contemporary château near Linfield College and downtown McMinnville, at 360 Wilson Street. Doris enjoys sharing with guests a love of spinning, weaving, and knitting with various wools collected from farms in the area; the couple used to raise sheep in eastern Oregon before moving to the valley. For information and reservations in one of the cozy guest rooms on the second floor or on the garden level—the largest suite offers a fireplace and a private deck overlooking the terraced gardens—contact the Steigers at (503) 472–0821. They can also offer helpful suggestions about which wineries and tasting rooms are currently open and will suggest historic walking tours around town. If Steiger Haus is filled, try **Springbrook Hazelnut Farm**—ask about the romantic Carriage House (503–538–4606); **The Partridge Farm**—with exotic game birds and gardens of perennials and vegetables (503–538–2050); or **Wine Country Farm**—with five varieties of growing grapes and Arabian horses (503–864–3446).

For dining, amenable choices are **Red Hills Cafe,** for fine Provincial dishes, 976 Highway 99W, Dundee (503–538–8224); **Tina's,** for Northwest and French cuisine, 760 Highway 99W, Dundee (503–538–8880); **Nick's Italian Cafe,** for northern Italian entrées, 521 E. Third Street, McMinnville (503–434–4471); **Sir Hinkleman's,** for good soups and salads, 729 E. Third Street, McMinnville (503–472–1309); and **Cornerstone Coffee,** for espresso and lattes, 403 E. Third Street, McMinnville (503–472–3267).

THE HEART OF THE VALLEY

Head toward the state capital by backtracking about 4 miles to Highway 221, turning south through Dayton into the heart of the Willamette Valley, and crossing the Willamette River on the ◆**Wheatland Ferry,** one of the last three ferries operating on this historic river. These old-fashioned contrivances are really just cable-operated barges. The ride is short, but you're treated to views upriver and downriver while lumbering across, and the kids will love it. Moreover, the price is right—about $1.00 for an auto. The two others in operation are the **Canby Ferry,** found just north and east of Canby, off Highway 99E,

Wheatland Ferry

and the **Buena Vista Ferry,** located about halfway between Salem and Albany, near the confluence of the Willamette and Santiam rivers. The usual hours are from 6:00 A.M. to 9:00 P.M. daily. Passengers on bicycles or on foot can usually ride free of charge.

In the early days of the territory, when competition for trade along the Willamette was keen, various trading-post sites in the valley sprang up on the banks of the river but were often washed away, as Champoeg was, by periodic floods. Just Albany and Corvallis have survived as good-size river towns. Before heading in that direction, though, detour at Salem for a walk through the lovely grounds of the state capitol. In early spring, dogwood, azaleas, and rhododendrons bloom about the well-manicured lawns that surround a large fountain. The setting also offers, from atop the capitol dome, a panoramic view of the city and the broad valley where the Calapooya Indians once lived. Inside the rotunda notice the large, colorful murals depicting historic scenes of the territory and Oregon's beginnings. There's a small visitors' center here where you can pick up local information.

Nearby at 1313 Mission Street, stroll through **Mission Mill Village,** which houses small shops, boutiques, and eateries, as well as the historic **Thomas Kay Woolen Mill,** in operation from 1889 to 1962. The restored mill now contains the Marion County Historical Society collections, and its displays show the process of changing fleece into fabric; the mill is open Tuesday through Saturday from 10:00 A.M. to 4:30 P.M. You can also join in a tour of the woolen mill and the array of historic houses at the village. Be sure to visit the circa 1841 **Jason Lee House,** the oldest remaining frame house in the Northwest and the structure that served as the territory's earliest Methodist mission. See, too, the **Pioneer Herb and Dye Garden's** accumulation of old-fashioned herbs and rare dye plants; the garden is located behind the Methodist Parsonage.

The woolen mill drew its power from **Mill Creek,** where there are shady places to feed the ducks and reflect upon the not-so-distant past. The Salem Visitors' Information Center (503–581–4235) is also located here at the village; the large parking area is a good place to leave your car or recreational vehicle while exploring the nearby historic areas by foot.

Just four blocks south, at Twelfth and Mission streets, flower lovers flock to see the marvelous gardens at **Bush House** and **Deepwood Estate Gardens.** At Bush House—an 1878, Italianate-style mansion built by Asahel Bush, a prominent politician and newspaperman—and at **Bush Pasture Park,** you can see and sniff a fine collection of old roses that bloom all summer. At Deepwood the 1894 Queen Anne mansion is surrounded by perennial, cottage-style, and formal gardens, and you can also browse through the adjacent greenhouse, filled with lush tropical palms, ferns, orchids, and begonias. Bush House is open June through August on Tuesday through Sunday from noon to 5:00 P.M. and is open September through May on the same days from 2:00 to 5:00 P.M.; call (503) 363–4714 for more information. Deepwood Estate is open May through September on Sunday and Monday and on Wednesday through Friday from noon to 4:30 P.M. (Saturdays are reserved for private weddings); call (503) 363–1825 for further information.

For a comfortable overnight stay, consider ♦ **Marquee House Bed and Breakfast,** an impressive Mt. Vernon Colonial–style house located bankside, on Mill Creek, just a few blocks from Deepwood Estate and the Bush House rose gardens. Innkeeper Rickie Hart offers five guest rooms decorated with collectibles and memorabilia to represent these famous old movies: *Auntie Mame, Blazing Saddles, Pillow Talk, Christmas in Connecticut,* and *Topper.* Breakfast, a hearty affair, is served in the sunny dining room or on the veranda, which overlooks the creek. You are invited to watch the evening movie and munch popcorn with other guests. For further information and reservations, contact Rickie Hart, 333 Wyatt Court NE, Salem 97301. The inn's phone number is (503) 391–0837. For eateries in the area, ask about **McGrath's Fish House, The Olive Garden, Union Oyster Bar,** and **Tudor Rose Tea Room.**

In addition to visiting Oregon's state capital, consider making another detour, this one from Interstate 5 east to **Silver Creek Falls State Park** and ♦ **Mt. Angel Abbey.** Located in the foothills of the Cascade Mountains, the park contains fourteen waterfalls interlaced with a maze of inviting trails in the cool forest—an especially good option on those occasional ninety-degree days in late summer. In autumn a colorful Oktoberfest is held near Mt. Angel.

The lovely abbey is situated on a hill the Indians called Tapalamaho, meaning "a place for communion with the Great Spirit." Swiss Benedictines established the monastery in 1883 and renamed the hill Mt. Angel. In addition to the monastery, the four-year seminary, a fine library (which is open to the public), and a museum, the abbey offers modest rooms and meals for folks who may have overdosed on work or simply have had too much civilization. The abbey also houses the **Russian Center Museum,** with its assortment of materials about the Russian Old Believers, who maintain a small community in the nearby French Prairie area. The abbey's library has an extensive Civil War and Swiss collection as well. For information about how to retreat to this lovely place, contact the staff at Mt. Angel Abbey, St. Benedict 97373 (503–845–3317).

Information about the annual **Oktoberfest** celebration, held in mid-September, can be obtained from the Silverton Visitors' Information Center, located in old Silverton depot at 424 S.

Water Street (503–873–5615). Silverton is about 14 miles northeast of Salem, via Highway 213. The abbey is located just 5 miles north of Silverton, and Silver Falls State Park lies about 15 miles south, on gently winding Highway 214. From the park head west back to Interstate 5, via Highways 214 and 22.

You can also head east into the high Cascades on Highway 22, going across 4,817-foot **Santiam Pass** and reaching central Oregon at Sisters, near the headwaters of the Metolius River. Santiam Pass, flanked by Mt. Washington and Mt. Jefferson, emerged as the main wagon route into the Willamette Valley from the high desert and rangeland areas; it was scouted up the South Santiam River by Andrew Wiley in 1859. Highway 20 from Albany roughly follows the old wagon route, connecting with Highway 22 near **Hoodoo Ski Area** at the top of the pass.

From Highway 22 wind west and south of Salem to Albany. Back in 1845, two enterprising Scots, Walter and Thomas Monteith, bought the Albany town site along the Willamette River, just 15 miles south of Independence, for $400 and a horse. Each of the three ◆ **Albany Historic Districts** offers fine examples of early nineteenth-century architecture. If possible, do the walking tour—you can park your car near the Visitors' Gazebo on Eighth Street. Some 350 homes—from Georgian Revival, Colonial Revival, and Federal to Classic, Stick, Gothic, and Italianate—have been restored and given status on the National Register of Historic Places. Next to Astoria on the north coast, Albany has one of the most impressive collections of such vintage structures in the state.

Before beginning the walking tour, linger at the gazebo to see old photos of Albany's beginnings and to enjoy a small garden graced by scented lavender, bright snapdragons, pale clematis, deep purple heliotrope, and double hollyhocks. For helpful maps and information about the historic districts and the annual **Victorian House Garden Tours,** contact the Albany Visitors' Information Center, 300 SW Second Ave (P.O. Box 965), Albany 97321. The telephone numbers are (503) 928–0911 or (800) 526–2256.

For a pleasant drive into the countryside, ask about the self-guided map to ten covered bridges in the surrounding area. At **Larwood Bridge,** circa 1939, crossing Crabtree Creek off Fish Hatchery Road, just east of Albany, enjoy a shady park near the swimming hole, along with the nostalgia of an old waterwheel that has been restored just downstream.

Visit one of the most recently renovated covered bridges just 14 miles west of Albany, in Corvallis, near the campus of Oregon State University. The bridge spans **Oak Creek** near Thirty-fifth Street and is now part of a popular bicycle and jogging path that meanders from here to nearby Philomath. The bridge, dismantled and mothballed in 1988, originally spanned the Long Tom River at Irish Bend, a tiny community near Monroe, just south of Corvallis. Local bridge buffs and an army of volunteers worked several weekends to reposition the old covered bridge and give it a new roof and fresh coats of white paint. Everyone turned out for the dedication in November 1989, including the OSU president, the Corvallis mayor, and all those hearty volunteers. For additional information about the area, contact the Corvallis Visitors' Information Center, 420 NW Second Avenue, Corvallis 97330 (503–757–1544).

For a pleasant midsummer afternoon outdoors, get directions at the Visitors' Center to **Avery Park and Rose Gardens.** Here you can sit amid a fine stand of towering redwoods near the extensive rose gardens while the kids somersault and play Frisbee on the enormous lawn. The roses bloom all summer and into fall.

Resuming the trail of the Calapooya Indians, continue south on old Highway 99W from Corvallis, past weathered barns, broad fields, and knolls dotted with oak, to the **William L. Finley National Wildlife Refuge.** Except for a few stragglers, the whole population of dusky Canada geese winters in the wide Willamette Valley and along the lower Columbia River, feeding on such winter grasses as ryegrass and fescue, as well as on the cereal grains and corn that are planted in fields near the refuge just for their use. Two additional refuges are located just north of Corvallis—**Ankeny Refuge** and **Baskett Slough Refuge.**

The 5,325-acre Finley Refuge was named for the early naturalist who persuaded President Theodore Roosevelt to create the first national wildlife refuges. Along the self-guided **Woodpecker Loop Trail,** open year-round, visitors can also see wood ducks, hooded mergansers (summer nesters), and ruffed grouse, as well as ring-necked pheasants, California and mountain quail, mourning doves, and black-tailed deer. Further information is available at the office of the refuge complex, 26208 Finley Refuge Road, Corvallis 97333 (503–757–7236).

From the wildlife refuge continue south on Highway 99W through Monroe and Junction City into the southernmost portion of the Willamette Valley, which includes Oregon's second-largest metropolitan area, Eugene-Springfield. This region also contains portions of three national forests—Siuslaw, Willamette, and Umpqua—as well as four high Cascades wilderness areas—French Pete, Three Sisters, Diamond Peak, and Mt. Washington.

Eugene, home of the University of Oregon, offers not only miles of jogging and bike paths but, especially for chocoholics, the **Euphoria Chocolate Company.** Hiding inside dark and light chocolate truffles the size of golf balls are tempting morsels of *ganache* or crème Parisienne, a rich creamy center that may be laced with amaretto, peppermint schnapps, pecan, toasted almond, or Grand Marnier, or try solid chocolate, milk chocolate, or coffee royal chocolate. You may also find owner Bob Bury there. Bob represents the third generation of chocolate makers, and his version is from an old family recipe handed down by his grandmother. If you can't eat the whole confection at one sitting, store the truffles in your cooler; they need to be refrigerated. The Euphoria Chocolate Company can be found in a small house-turned-store at 6 W. Seventeenth Street, just off Willamette Street a few blocks south of the downtown area; the phone number is (503) 343–9223.

Then, too, you could make a pit stop at **Starbuck's Coffee House,** nearby at W. Eighteenth near Willamette Street, for steaming Coffee of the Day, foamy lattes, and pungent espresso as well as delicious scones, muffins, and cookies. Actually, you can find the now familiar green-and-white Starbuck's sign in major cities and towns throughout Oregon and Washington (where the regional espresso mania began a few years ago).

Of course you could always jog or bicycle off the extra calories on the area's network of trails and paths, but **canoeing on the Millrace** might offer a more inviting, less strenuous alternative. Constructed in 1851 by Hilyard Shaw to generate power for the flour mills, woolen mills, and sawmills lining its banks, the narrow stream bubbles up from a pipe that diverts water from the nearby Willamette River; the Millrace then flows through the blackberry vines and ambles behind a number of motels and eateries just across Franklin Boulevard from the University of Oregon campus. For many decades it's been the site of college pranks and canoe fêtes—often occurring under a full moon. When the water iced over during winter, everyone skated on it, and by the end of the 1920s—when the mills switched to electricity—the Millrace had become the recreational hub of the city.

In the days of the canoe fêtes, around 1915, barges and even empty oil drums were transformed into everything from water lilies to seashells. Colored lights were strung along the water, and bleachers were set up along the shore. The boys would swim alongside the floats, while the girls held court on top. Although such fêtes on the Millrace are a tradition of the past, you can still enjoy paddling along its lazy, 2-mile-long, backyard journey to Ferry Street, where the water rejoins the Willamette River. Park close to Franklin Boulevard and near the bridge that crosses over to the **Alton Baker Park** nature trails, and enjoy sitting in the sun or picnicking on the grassy banks in the company of friendly quacking ducks that will eagerly chase after your bread scraps. For current information about renting canoes, call the Canoe Shack (located near the bridge) at (503) 346–4386, River Runner's Supply at (503) 343–6883, or contact the city's Outdoor Recreation Office at River House (503–687–5329).

If you plan to stay overnight in the area, consider calling Irma and Don Mode in Junction City to see whether an antiques-filled guest room is available at ◆ **Black Bart Bed and Breakfast.** Black Bart isn't a nefarious outlaw relative; rather, he's a famous National Grand Champion mammoth donkey who loves to have his ears scratched and who often takes guests for a ride in the Modes' antique shay, an open two-wheeled carriage.

Nip and Tuck, a friendly pair of Belgian mules, often take guests for rides as well in a 1906 farm wagon or in a fancy light-spring wagon. The farmhouse was built sometime in the 1880s, and the original land claim dates to 1861. Renovated by Don and Irma with the help of friends and relatives, the farmhouse is once again filled with sunlight, and you can choose from two cozy guest rooms on the second floor that feature handmade quilts, milk-glass lamps, stuffed animals, antique dolls, and yes, donkey memorabilia.

Nearby are antiques shops and golf courses, as well as wineries, dairies, and museums to tour and visit. For further information, including dates and events planned for the annual **Scandinavian Festival** held in August, contact the innkeepers at 94125 Love Lake Road, Junction City 97448 (503–998–1904).

A leisurely and pleasant drive from Junction City loops west along pastoral Highway 36, across Bear Creek, along Long Tom River, around **Triangle Lake,** through Deadwood and Swisshome to Mapleton and the tidewaters at the mouth of the Siuslaw River at Florence, and then back to Eugene on Highway 126, through Walton, Elmira, and Veneta. Linger at Triangle Lake or stop along the way and pick out a river-worn rock to sit on. While listening to the singing of the streams and rivers, relax into nature's setting and feel the warmth of the afternoon sun—maybe even take a snooze. Along the way are several waysides and picnic areas, some with boat landings, but no campgrounds on this particular route. When you get back to Eugene, stop for lunch, a late-afternoon snack, or dinner at **Zenon's Cafe** downtown, on the corner of Pearl and Broadway streets, or at the nearby **Fifth Street Public Market,** at the corner of Pearl and Fifth streets.

In the shadowy coolness of groves of mature filbert (hazelnut) trees planted by pioneer farmer George Dorris in 1903, you and the kids will also enjoy visiting the historic ◆**Dorris Ranch** in nearby Springfield. Listed on the National Register of Historic Places and in the process of becoming a **living-history program,** the ranch still produces a good-size crop of the small, round hazelnuts each fall. Actually, farmer Dorris would probably be surprised to learn that less than a hundred years after he planted those first trees, the Willamette Valley produces nearly 98 percent of the world's commercial hazelnuts.

The living-history program developed by the Willamalane Park and Recreation District offers workshops in tree maintenance, old orchard restoration, and nature photography, along with guided walks of the ranch. Meet at the barn for tours, which take place from April through October; call (503) 726–4325 for additional information and to arrange for a large-group tour. To locate Dorris Ranch from Interstate 105, just off Interstate 5 at the Springfield exit, take the Springfield City Center exit and drive south on Pioneer Parkway. A mile or so past the downtown area, where the street turns right, continue straight on the gravel road, following signs to the ranch (Pioneer Parkway turns into Second Street).

CENTRAL CASCADES

If you pass through the Eugene-Springfield area during September or October, consider taking a walking tour of the **University of**

Oregon campus before heading into the mountains.The outing provides a pleasant visual overdose of autumn hues clustered on a wide variety of well-established native and non-native tree species, and you'll find plenty of places to park in and around the campus.

Then head about 70 miles farther on the trail of glorious autumn foliage by continuing east from Springfield via Highway 126, to access the ◆**McKenzie Pass Scenic Drive.** After driving through the tiny communities of Vida, Blue River, and McKenzie Bridge—each hugs the banks of the McKenzie River like a dedicated trout angler—turn onto Highway 242, just east of the McKenzie Ranger Station, for one of the best displays of fall colors in the region.

That characteristic nip in the air signals the return of another season in the Northwest woods, and autumn declares its arrival with leaves turned bright crimson, vibrant orange, and vivid yellow. On the quiet winding road that loops and twists about 20 miles to the top of McKenzie Pass, soft breezes whisper through dark green Douglas fir and stir the strikingly colored leaves of big leaf maple, vine maple, alder, and mountain ash.

You're in the **Willamette National Forest** now—the largest of eighteen forests within Oregon and Washington and one of the largest in the United States. The original incentive for finding a route across the Cascades in this area was the discovery of gold in Idaho more than a century ago. Captain Felix Scott and a couple of colleagues, John Cogswell and John Templeman Craig, formed a party at Eugene to deliver supplies to the Idaho mining area. Using established Indian trails, they chopped through the tangled forest in the fall of 1862 with a party of 250 workers, more than a hundred ox teams and wagons, and some 850 head of cattle and horses. Under the auspices of his firm, the McKenzie Salt Springs and Deschutes Wagon Road Company, John Craig collected tolls at McKenzie Bridge until 1891. He lived nearby for many years and is buried at the summit.

Sometime around 1810 an automobile chugged over the summit, probably with extra fuel, water, and a supply of axes and saws to remove limbs and trees that seemed always to plague early travelers on the rutted, bumpy gravel and dirt roads. You will reach the top of the 5,325-foot pass with relative ease, however, and can detour into the parking area to walk stone steps up to the ◆**Dee Wright Observatory.** From this towerlike stone structure, constructed in the early 1930s by the Civilian Conservation

Corps, you can peer through eleven narrow windows, each focused on a particular mountain peak; the peak's name and distance from the viewpoint are carved into the stone.

To the southeast are Belknap Crater, Mt. Washington, the North and Middle Sister, and Mt. Scott; Mt. Jefferson and Mt. Hood hover over lesser peaks to the north. If time allows, walk the 2-mile trail—it's part of the Pacific Crest National Scenic Trail—up **Little Belknap Crater** to see fissures, lava tunnels, and spatter cones. Like Lava Cast Forest near Bend, it's an intriguing, close-up encounter with those massive lava fields of the high central Cascades, which cover thousands of acres with at least three layers of the rough black stuff.

The gray-andesite, snowy peaks of the most ancient flow are scored with glaciers and strewn with volcanic dust, cinders, and debris of the second flow. Next are the layers of black or burnt-umber lava of the third disturbance. Although the volcanoes are quiet now, geologists believe the fires deep inside Oregon's Cascade crest are just napping and may someday erupt again, as did Mt. Saint Helens to the north, in Washington, in May 1980. The McKenzie Ranger Station will have current weather and road information for the area; maps of the nearby McKenzie River National Recreation Trail, which is especially suited to beginning hikers and families with young children; and directions to nearby Forest Service campgrounds. Located on Highway 126, the ranger station is open from 8:00 A.M. to 4:30 P.M. on weekdays; its phone number is (503) 822–3381. *Note:* Highway 242 is closed by snow during winter months.

You can also call the folks at **Belknap Springs Lodge** to reserve room in their historic, refurbished lodge on the banks of the McKenzie River a couple of miles from the ranger station. A few small cabins—bring your own bedding—and camping/recreational vehicle spaces are also available, all within walking distance of the hot mineral springs swimming pool. You can also walk to a picturesque section of the **McKenzie River Recreation Trail** from the upper campground and enjoy a short walk within earshot of the bubbling river.

The many mineral springs in the area were long known to Indian peoples, who believed they held restorative and healing powers. Trails led to secret places where the Indians stopped regularly to take baths in the warm waters. Belknap Hot Springs, discovered by R. S. Belknap around 1869, was a longtime favorite of families living in the valley.

The lodge was built just across the river from the mineral springs, and by 1910, a daily motor stage from Eugene had been established—the trip on the original dirt and gravel road took a whole day. During the season of 1890, some 700 lodge guests were registered, at a cost of $15.00 per week; one could tent camp at a weekly rate of $1.50. Then, after having been in the same family for seventy years, the lodge was sold, in 1975, to Jim Nation, a retired Army Corps of Engineer dredge-ship captain; before his purchase, the lodge had been closed for some ten years and had fallen into disrepair. Restoring and adding rooms to the original lodge took Jim nearly three years, including cleaning and shoring up the large swimming pool.

On your visit you'll notice billows of steam rising from the hot springs on the far side of the McKenzie River; the 130-degree mineral water is piped across the lodge and pool. Most hot springs contain about two dozen different minerals—from potash and arsenic, silica and potassium, chlorine and calcium to sodium, sulphuric acid, and bicarbonic acid. The water, from deep underground where temperatures are scalding, rises along cracks or fissures in places of faulted and folded rock. The mineral water is cooled to a temperature of about 102 degrees in the swimming pool and is perfect for soaking one's weary bones at the end of a day of hiking and exploring the area. For further information and reservations, contact the staff at Belknap Springs Lodge, McKenzie Bridge 97413 (503–822–3512).

Playing hide-and-seek with Highway 126, the snow-fed McKenzie River has long been known by lovers of fishing. According to lively accounts from old newspapers of the early 1900s, "wet flies were disdained by the swiftly traveling denizens of the rapids and many misses suffered before anglers acquired the knack of handling the rod properly . . . whether trout bite or not, there are times when a fisherman must stop fishing and tell fish stories." For current regulations and angler's licenses, stop at one of the local grocery stores in Vida, Leaburg, Blue River, or McKenzie Bridge. You can also contact the Oregon Department of Fish and Wildlife for helpful maps, brochures, and current regulations: 2501 SW First Avenue, Portland 97207 (503–229–5403).

For information about guided river fishing in the well-known ◆**McKenzie River Driftboats,** as well as about guided rafting trips, contact the Eugene-Springfield Visitors' Information Center, 305 W. Seventh Street, Eugene 97440 (503–484–5307 or 800–452–3670 in Oregon and 800–547–5445 outside Oregon).

A final detour into this valley section of the high Cascades is accessed via Highway 58, just south of Eugene and winding up to the community of **Oakridge.** Along the way notice the Southern Pacific Railroad tracks, a historic transportation link to the upper Willamette area that has operated since 1912. In the early 1930s as many as five passenger trains passed through Oakridge each day, with stops at Fields, McCredie Springs, Cascade Summit, and Crescent Lake on the east side of the pass. Rotary snowplows, mounted on the trains, kept the Cascade line open during the winter, and the train crews stopped at a cook house at the summit for hot meals.

In good weather a popular excursion in those early days was to get off the train at Diamond Creek, hike down a trail to ◆**Salt Creek Falls,** enjoy a picnic beneath tall firs, and then take the next train back home. The falls are located about 8 miles up Highway 58 east of Oakridge, and there you can also hike a short trail to this spectacular, frothy ribbon, which cascades some 286 feet down into a small canyon. These are the second-highest falls in the state; two other lovely falls, **Sahalie** and **Koosah,** can be visited in the McKenzie Bridge area, just above the ranger station, off Highway 126.

Next continue east to the 5,128-foot summit, **Willamette Pass,** to see one of the state's oldest ski areas. Of course the original rope tow built by Roy Temple and fellow ski enthusiasts from Oakridge in the 1940s is now gone, but in its place rises a chair lift that carries a new crop of skiers nearly a mile to the top of 6,666-foot Eagle Peak. Roy and his wife, Edna, ran the original ski area for a number of years and lived at Cascade Summit, at the west end of nearby Odell Lake. Edna remembers making and serving chili, hot dogs, cupcakes, and coffee from the ski shack, with a roaring bonfire out in front. She still lives in Oakridge and, still spry in her seventies, volunteers at the **Oakridge Pioneer Museum,** where visitors can browse through photographs and memorabilia from the not-so-distant past. Located at 76433 Pine Street, Oakridge 97463, the museum is open on Saturday from 1:00 to 4:00 P.M. by appointment. Call (503) 782–3904 to reach the curator, Aulene Owens, for further information.

For an overnight stay just east of the summit, at an elevation of 4,800 feet, check with owners John and Janet Milandin at **Odell Lake Lodge,** located at the sunny southeast corner of the lake. There is moorage space at the marina, and motorboats, canoes, rowboats, and small sailboats are available to rent by the hour or day. In summer and fall anglers fish for Kokanee salmon, Mackinaw lake trout, and native rainbow trout on the 5-mile-long, 300-foot-deep lake; during winter cross-country skiers and snow bunnies flock to the area from the valley.

The small restaurant in the lodge is open daily, year-round, and serves all three meals. For further information and reservations, contact the Milandins at Odell Lake Lodge, P.O. Box 72, Crescent Lake 97425 (503–433–2540).

COVERED BRIDGE COUNTRY

Continuing south on Interstate 5, exit at Cottage Grove and, bearing to the east past the Village Green resort on Row River Road, stop at the Forest Service Ranger Station to pick up a copy of the self-guided *Tour of the Golden Past.* From Row River Road, take back roads past vintage covered bridges into the **Bohemia Mine** area, reading colorful descriptions of the historic mines and seeing the sights along the way.

With a radiator full of water and good brakes, adventurous travelers can negotiate the narrow, winding gravel road to **Fairview Peak** and **Musick Mine,** at the top of 5,933-foot Bohemia Mountain. On a clear day Mt. Shasta can be seen to the south, the gossipy Three Sisters Mountains to the north, and the Coast Range to the west. Along the 70-mile loop drive are other places to stop as well.

Although some 400 miners once called the Calapooya Mountains in this area home, now gentle breezes rattle broken, rusted hinges and scuttle through a fallen-down cook house or blacksmith shop or remnants of an old hotel or store. The mines flourished from 1890 until 1910, with some activity after World War I, but most of the mines have given way to wind, rain, snow, and time. Community members want to preserve some of the old buildings near Musick Mine, where, in the old days, it took six to eight horses from eight to ten hours to pull a load of supplies and mining equipment up Hardscrabble Grade, the steep, 6-mile trail.

Today smooth country roads reach into the Bohemia mining country, wrapping around green hills and pastures where woolly sheep and multicolored cows graze peacefully in the sun. *Note:* Even though a shack may look long forgotten and deserted, it may actually be someone's headquarters for mining exploration or assessment work; the mines are on private land and are not to be disturbed by travelers. Check at the ranger station in Cottage Grove if you're interested in public gold-panning areas—there are several in the immediate area.

A wagon road was the first main route into the Row River area; it wound along the river through Culp Creek to ◆ **Red Bridge,** a covered bridge built in 1879. In the surrounding Cottage Grove–Eugene–Springfield area, it's possible to explore nearly twenty of the fifty-three covered bridges still standing in the state. Calling forth a bit of horse-and-buggy nostalgia or images of kids with fishing poles and cans of worms, most covered bridges are under the protection of local historical societies. Although most are no longer for public use, a few do remain open to automobile traffic and, of course, to artists, photography buffs, and kids with fishing poles. In Cottage Grove the **Covered Bridge Festival** is celebrated in mid-September.

From exposed trusses and rounded portals, to Gothic-, portal-, or louvered-style windows, to tin or shingled roofs, the covered bridges in this area are more numerous than in any other section of the state; five are in the immediate Cottage Grove area, and four are still in the active use for automobiles, bicyclers, and hikers. The longest covered bridge in the state is **Office Bridge,** spanning 180 feet across a millpond off the North Fork of the Willamette River; the shortest, at just 39 feet, is **Lost Creek Bridge,** located in southern Oregon.

In the 1930s there were more than 300 covered bridges in the state, but by the 1950s their numbers had dwindled to fewer than 140. The **Covered Bridge Society of Oregon** is dedicated to preserving and restoring the remaining bridges and also promotes the study of the bridges' history and unique construction. The group offers covered-bridge tours, picnics, quarterly newsletters, slide talks, and historical information about the bridges, and it sells memorabilia as well. If you'd like to join the ranks of enthusiastic volunteers and covered-bridge buffs, contact the Covered Bridge Society of Oregon at 3940 Courtney Lane SE,

Red Bridge

Salem 97302, or call Bill Cockrell at (503) 399–0436. A helpful map and brochure showing all fifty-three bridge locations in twelve different areas of the state can be obtained at the Cottage Grove Visitors' Information Center, 710 Row River Road (P.O. Box 587), Cottage Grove 97424 (503–942–2411).

For easy hiking into grassy meadows of alpine wildflowers in July and August, near Cottage Grove, try the **June Mountain Trail,** the **Adams Mountain Trail,** or the **Hardesty Trail**—maps and information are available at the ranger station. Keep alert, too, for some of the forty kinds of edible wild berries that grow in the region. Tiny wild blackberries ripen in August, salal berries are abundant in forested areas, and the Oregon grape berries are plentiful in late summer and fall. All make delicious jams and jellies, and all were used by the Native American peoples as well.

In early spring you can see waves of purple camas that carpet the swales along Interstate 5 between Creswell and Cottage Grove. Long ago the Indians gathered the tiny bulbs of the purple camas and steamed them in large pits lined with heated rocks and wet grass, covered over with hides to hold in the heat. Looking like citron and tasting much like sweet potatoes, the steamed bulbs were dried and stored for winter food. Camas mixed with ground tarweed seeds made a tasty native dish. Cattail and other roots and bulbs were also dried and ground into flour, and wide skunk cabbage leaves provided handy wrappings.

In mid-July, Cottage Grove celebrates **Bohemia Mining Days** with a tour of historic homes, an old-timers' breakfast, fiddlers' contests, and the Grand Miners Parade down Main Street; the Prospector's Breakfast at the top of Bohemia Mountain usually ends the four-day celebration. For additional information, including bed-and-breakfast lodgings, contact the Cottage Grove Visitors' Information Center. You can also see Bohemia mining memorabilia at the **Cottage Grove Historical Museum,** housed in the circa 1897, octagonal, former church building located at Birch and H streets. The museum is open mid-June through Labor Day on Wednesday through Sunday from 1:00 to 5:00 P.M. Call (503) 942–8175 for additional information.

Travel Planning Resources and Maps

Oregon Tourism Division, 775 Summer Street NE, Salem, OR 97310. Telephone number: (800) 547–7842 Monday through Friday, 8:00 A.M. to 5:00 P.M.

Oregon Parks and Recreation Department, 525 Trade Street SE, Salem, OR 97310. Call (503) 378–6305. Campsite information and reservation telephone number: (503) 238–7488.

U.S. Forest Service campgrounds and hiking trails information: Recreation Director, U.S. Forest Service, 333 SW First Avenue, Portland, OR 97204. Telephone number: (503) 326–2877.

U.S. Bureau of Land Management campgrounds and trails information: BLM, OR/WA State Office, P.O. Box 2965, Portland, OR 97208. Telephone number: (503) 280–7001 Monday through Friday, 7:30 A.M. to 4:00 P.M.

Army Corps of Engineers campgrounds and lakes information: P.O. Box 7870, Portland OR 97208. Telephone number: (503) 326–3768.

Oregon Coast Visitors' Association, P.O. Box 4, Lincoln City, OR 97367. Telephone number: (800) 858–8598.

Southwestern Oregon Visitors Association, P.O. Box 1645, Medford, OR 97501. Telephone numbers: (503) 779–4691 or (800) 448–4856 (USA).

Central Oregon Recreation Association, P.O. Box 230, 63085 North Highway 97, Bend, OR 97709. Telephone number: (503) 382–8334.

Eastern Oregon Visitors' Association, 490 Campbell Street, Baker City, OR 97814. Telephone numbers: (503) 523–3356 or (800) 523–1235 (USA and Canada).

North Central Oregon Tourism Association, 901 E. Second Street, The Dalles, OR 97058. Telephone number: (503) 296–6616.

Northwest Oregon Visitors' Association, 26 SW Salmon Street, Portland, OR 97204. Telephone numbers: (503) 222–2223 or (800) 962–3700 (outside Oregon).

Columbia River Gorge National Scenic Area information, 902 Wasco Avenue, Hood River, OR 97031. Telephone number: (503) 386–2333.

Mt. Hood Recreation Association, 65000 East Highway 26, P.O. Box 342, Welches, OR 97067. Telephone number: (503) 622–3162.

Willamette Valley Visitors' Association, 300 SW Second Avenue, P.O. Box 965, Albany, OR 97321. Telephone number: (800) 526–2256 (USA).

National Park Service, recreation information for Pacific Northwest Region, 83 S. King Street, Suite 212, Seattle, WA 98104. Telephone numbers: (206) 220–7450 or (503) 594–2211.

Helpful telephone numbers

Oregon Highway, Mountain Pass and Road Conditions: (503) 976–7277 or (503) 889–3999, twenty-four hours
Weather Information: (503) 236–7575
Road Construction Information: (503) 378–6318
Forest Fire Information: (503) 378–2560
Fishing and Hunting Licenses: (503) 229–5403
Oregon Guides and Packers: (503) 683–9552
Oregon Marine Board: (503) 378–8587
State Police: (503) 378–3720

INDEX

Acknowledgments

Special thanks to the following friends, innkeepers, historians, and fellow writers for providing information, helpful research assistance, and inspiration: Jack and Bea Rawls, Katrina and Doug Haines, Lee and Matt Utal, Elaine Shanafelt, Mary Lou Cavendish, Cynthia Withee, Claire Met, Don Williams, Melody and Bob Johnson, Sara Jameson, and Marilyn McFarlane.

About the Author

Myrna Oakley has traveled the byways of the Northwest and western British Columbia since 1970, always with a camera in hand and an inquisitive eye for natural and scenic areas, as well as for interesting people, intriguing inns, gardens, and places with historical character and significance.

In addition to *Oregon: Off the Beaten Path,* she has written *Public and Private Gardens of the Northwest* and *Bed and Breakfast Northwest.* She also teaches about the business of freelance writing, novel writing, and travel writing at Marylhurst College, near Portland.

About the Illustrator

Elizabeth Neilson Walker lives in Portland and operates her own graphic arts business. She also illustrates fiction and nonfiction books for children and adults. Her dream is to live in a beach house on the Oregon coast.